W9-BAR-670

AMERICA'S VANISHING FOLKWAYS

AMERICA'S

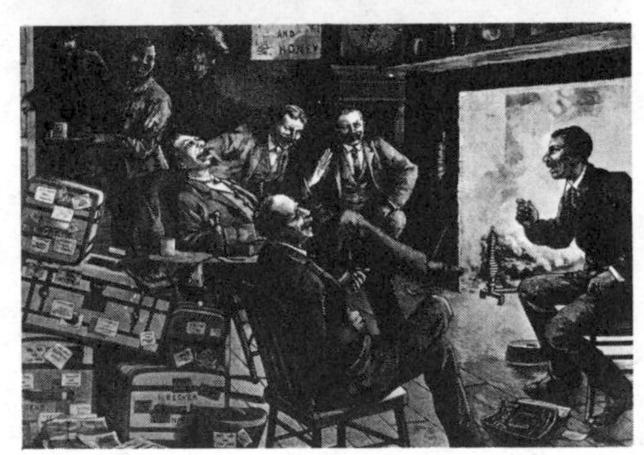

BY
EVERETT B. WILSON

VANISHING FOLKWAYS

New York: A. S. Barnes and Co. • London: Thomas Yoseloff Ltd

Library of Congress Catalogue Card Number: 65-14238

A. S. Barnes and Co., Inc.
South Brunswick, N.J.

Thomas Yoseloff Ltd
18 Charing Cross Road
London W.C.2, England

6240

Printed in the United States of America

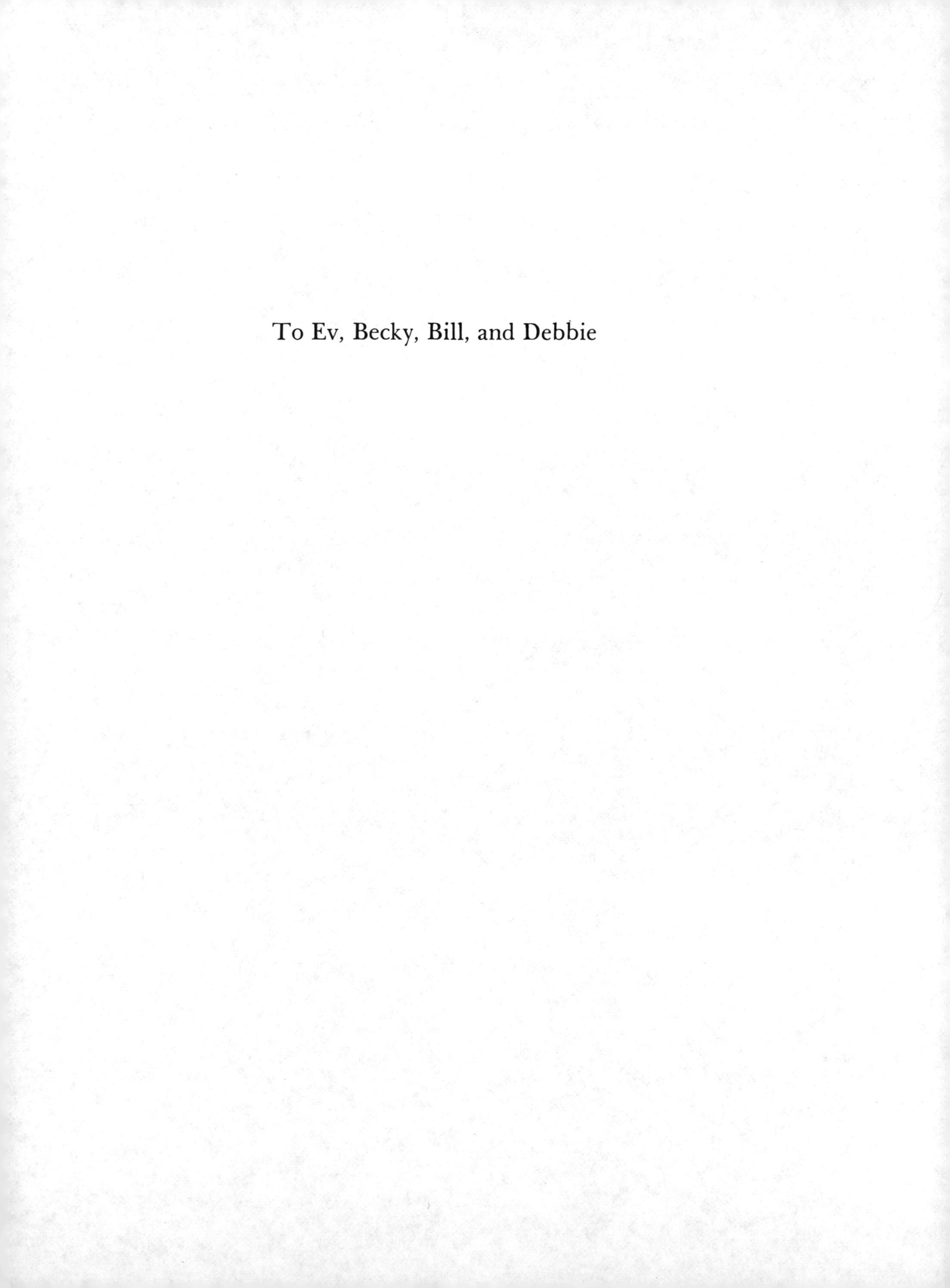

To Ev, Becky, Bill, and Debbie

Acknowledgments

The author is indebted to Miss Marian V. Bell, of the Enoch Pratt Free Library, Baltimore, Maryland, and to Mrs. Helen R. Thompson and Mr. Raymond T. Elgin, Jr., of the District of Columbia Public Library, for valuable assistance in reproducing many of the illustrations appearing in this book, and to the following for assistance with photographs:

Mr. and Mrs. Allison H. Chapin

Mrs. Herbert S. Colton, Bethesda, Maryland

Mrs. Frederick Gilpin, Olney, Maryland

Mr. and Mrs. Mahlon Kirk IV, Sandy Spring, Maryland

Mrs. Albert R. Martin, Northfield, Illinois

Mrs. Richard E. Robbins, Alexandria, Louisiana

Mr. and Mrs. Robert Warner, Washington, Connecticut

Mrs. John W. Watson, Washington, D.C.

In addition, the author received special editorial assistance from Miss Maren Mortensen, Alexandria, Virginia.

Contents

Introduction

This book describes and pictures many of the sweeping changes that have been taking place in our customs and manners as new inventions, new attitudes, and new ideas have come along through the years and as our society has become better educated and more sophisticated.

The advent of the automobile, for example, brought a host of new customs and eliminated many old ones. Whereas it formerly was incorrect for a gentleman to sit next to a lady in a carriage, he must now sit next to her in an auto because today's passenger cars do not have facing seats. And a gentleman no longer is expected to hand a lady her fan, parasol, and shawl before starting a drive out to the country, because she no longer requires these accessories.

The introduction of air conditioning has made it unnecessary for a lady to carry a fan into a formal dinner, and now that many ladies smoke and accept strong beverages, gentlemen do not ordinarily retire alone to a smoking room for cigars and brandy after dinner.

The introduction of the fork to the dining table has made it unnecessary to eat with one's fingers or knife and, thus, has reduced the number of napkins needed on the table.

Each year a few of our old, traditional folkways are dropped and new ones are adopted to replace them. The installation of inside plumbing and automatic water heaters, for example, has made it practical to bathe every day, or at least several times a week, instead of only on Saturday night. Revisions in our concepts of feminine modesty have led to radical changes in feminine attire, especially at the beach or pool and in other athletic activities.

The introduction of the telephone for easy communication with one's friends and acquaintances has all but eliminated the practice of leaving calling cards after one has been a guest in a lady's home. The replacement of kerosene lamps by more convenient lighting has done away with the daily tasks of cleaning and refilling the lamps and cleaning the chimneys.

We no longer go courting with horse and buggy or elope on horseback, and fathers nowadays seldom go through the formality of giving a dowry to the groom when their daughters marry.

A better understanding of human psychology and our growing humanitarianism have done away with most of the cruel and inhuman punishments that our courts once called for and that our society inflicted on wrongdoers.

These and many other changing customs are described and pictured in illustrations copied from periodicals published in the 1870's, 1880's, and 1890's, including *Century Magazine, Scribner's Monthly Magazine, Leslie's Popular Monthly, Frank Leslie's Illustrated Newspaper, Harper's Illustrated Weekly,* and other contemporary periodicals. Most of the illustrations were created by the foremost artists of the day and reproduced by woodcuts. The author is deeply indebted to those masters and their publishers.

The original photographs were made by the author with the valued assistance of individuals named in the list of acknowledgments.

E.B.W.

Bethesda, Maryland

AMERICA'S VANISHING FOLKWAYS

AN ELOPEMENT—THE GETAWAY.

1. Our Personal Lives

Courtship and Marriage

Few of our customs have undergone greater change than those surrounding courtship and marriage. Both are far more informal than in colonial times and more free and unimpeded, for that matter, than in the early part of the twentieth century.

To show what young people were up against in the early days, the Puritans had a law which required a young man to get express permission from a girl's father before he could start to pay addresses to her. If he so much as wrote to her, winked at her, held clandestine meetings, or sent her a gift or valentine, he was subject to penalties as severe as whipping.

And even when the permission to court was received, dating was a lot different than we know it today. Houses being small, with only one room—usually the kitchen—where all the family gathered in the evening, the young people had relatively little privacy. One way to gain it was by using a whispering stick, a long tube which one of the young people could talk into while the other listened, with little danger of being overheard.

Another source of privacy came from the practice of bundling, also known as questing and tarrying, in which two young people shared the same bed in the after-dinner hours, though fully dressed and blanketed and often with a board between them. Until around 1800, this practice was justified even by some rigid-minded parents on the grounds that it saved fuel on bitter-cold winter nights. The young gentleman stayed the night or else went home when the time came to retire. The practice was bitterly condemned by some people and just as emotionally favored by others, who felt that bundling was safer than sitting side-by-side on a sofa.

Later on came the chaperone system under which a girl of "good breeding" was never alone in the company of a boy, except when her parents or a chaperone

AN ELOPEMENT—THE INTERRUPTION.

ARRANGING A DOWRY.

A PARENTAL CHOICE.

CHILDHOOD LOVERS.

CARRYING HER BOOKS.

LOVE IN THE FIELDS.

A LOVERS' SPAT.

A COURTING STICK.

AN UNDECIDED MISS.

were present to make sure decorum was observed. There were ways to evade a chaperone, at least for brief periods, but young people regarded them as a nuisance nevertheless. In this connection, Emily Post said, very wisely, "A very young married woman gadding about without her husband is not a proper chaperone." Even when a chaperone was not provided, young people were expected to observe certain rules that are passé today.

One book said that a fiancé never stays after ten o'clock unless present for a family visit, and added that a two-hour visit with one's fiancée is quite long enough. Moreover, an escort never accepts an invitation to enter a lady's home after a ball. In that connection, Emily Post said in a rather late edition of her book on etiquette that "it still is considered an unforgiveable breach of etiquette to allow a young girl to sit up late with a young man—or a group of them—after her elders have gone to bed. On returning home from a party, she must not invite or allow a man to 'come in for a while.' Even her fiancé must bid her goodnight at the door if the hour is late, and someone ought always to sit up or

A BUTCHER'S WEDDING MARCH.

A WIFE FOR SALE.

SELECTING A WIFE AT THE BOAT.

get up to let her in. No young girl ought to let herself in with a latch-key if it can be avoided."

The leading books on decorum also advised that no lady ever permits a gentleman other than a near relative or old friend of the family to defray the cost of theater tickets or pay for a refreshment or vehicle when she is out under his protection. How things have changed!

Among former courtship practices we seldom hear of today are carrying a girl's books home from school (this is not necessary for those millions who ride on school buses), giving the bridegroom a dowry, and going on spooning, necking, or petting parties. There now are other names for such activities.

The young man of fifty years ago used to hire a horse and buggy to take his girl for a drive in the country on a summer's evening or Sunday afternoon, whereas today he borrows a friend's car if he hasn't one himself.

Completely out of style is the marriage of convenience in which a girl married a man merely because he was willing to support or pay the debts of her family. Today parents no longer select the mates for their children and are less inclined to forbid marriage, with the result that elopements are less frequent.

In Pennsylvania, it was at one time the custom for the bride and groom to have open house for several days after their wedding, with swarms of friends around almost continously, kissing the bride and drinking punch. In some cases, the lucky couple gave a tea party every afternoon for a week, with the bridesmaids and ushers constantly in attendance.

Now that marriageable women are more plentiful, we no longer hear of a man meeting a boatload of immigrants for the purpose of selecting a wife before other single men get a chance at her. Nor do we hear of a husband selling his wife when he becomes displeased with her. This belongs in the past along with plural marriages.

BRINGING HOME HIS FIFTH WIFE.

READY FOR THE BIG WAVES.

A PORTABLE BATHHOUSE.

Seashore Bathing

Since swimming pools are a relatively new development, outdoor bathing until not too many years ago was restricted to the oceans, lakes, ponds, and inland streams. At the old swimming holes patronized in various rural places, bathing attire was most informal, consisting either of nothing at all or else an old pair of short pants or drawers, or a dress of some type.

At the more fashionable ocean beaches, however, things were different. Until the twentieth century was well launched, men and women alike were attired in a most modest manner when they appeared on the beach. The men customarily wore a pair of knee-length woolen bathing drawers and a high-necked, half-sleeved jersey. Older men wore shoes and socks and usually a hat.

Milady not only wore bathing stockings and shoes, but also drawers that met the stockings well below the knees and a top garment, usually made of gray or dark blue flannel, in the form of a sack which hung loose or had a yoke waist, fitted in with a belt and falling halfway between the knees and ankle. A small close-fitting hat also was worn. Only when going skiing or tobogganing today does a lady appear in public so completely covered.

The term bathing beauty was almost unheard of in those days because there was not enough beauty on display to justify the term. However, the men were not slow to appreciate a nicely turned ankle on the beach, since such a sight seldom was visible on the streets.

Among the more famous female bathers in our history were Annette Kellerman, who introduced the one-piece swimming suit for women, and September Morn, the calendar girl, who wore none at all.

BATHING WITHOUT STOCKINGS.

KEEPING OUT OF THE SUN.

THE WHOLE FAMILY AT THE BEACH.

BATHING IN THE RAW.

Home Bathing

The traditional Saturday night bath is a thing of the past now that almost every home has running water and water heaters which make it easy to bathe more often. But when the water had to be carried in from the outside pump, heated on the kitchen stove, carried to the wooden or galvanized bathing tub, and then carried outside again, a pailful at a time, one bath a week seemed plenty.

Moreover, as recently as 1870 there was medical advice supporting less frequent bathing. During the summer, individuals were advised to take a warm bath once a week, a douche or hip bath each morning, and a sponge bath just before retiring. Presumably one's own judgment was to prevail in winter. It was emphasized that the feet should be washed at least once a week.

One authority warned his readers to avoid a bath if fatigued or overheated, to wet the head with cold water before stepping into the bath, and to sponge the pit of the stomach first after entering the tub.

The vigorous use of a hair glove or "electric" brush was urged while bathing. The advisor said that a showerbath could not be recommended for indiscriminate use, "since it can be endured only by the most rigorous constitution." He presumably was thinking of a cold water shower. Lack of a built-in bathtub was no excuse for not bathing, because a large piece of oil-cloth could be spread on the floor and the individual could bathe out of a pail, a large tin tub, or a basin of water.

Owners of beards were told that their beards should be washed and dusted at least twice a day, since they were likely to pick up dust, food particles, and other impurities.

Men who shaved themselves—two shaves a week were considered ample—often had a special stand to hold the razor, a mirror, comb and brush, and other articles including a shaving mug and shaving brush.

To promote good health, air baths were recommended. They consisted of remaining unclothed for some time after

A SHAVING STAND.

SUPERVISED WASHING.

AN OLD WASHSTAND.

bathing, "while performing such duties of the toilet as can be carried out in that condition."

When one was washing rather than bathing, the wash bowl and pitcher were employed. There might be a set in each bedroom or else one set in a hallway for all the family. The bowl and pitcher, plus a soap dish and slop jar, were kept on a washstand or commode. The water poured from the pitcher into the basin was discarded into the slop jar after it had been used, and then the slop jar was carried outside to be emptied.

Among the duties which might be performed during an air bath was cleaning one's teeth. Very sparing use of tooth washes or powders was recommended. Instead, the preferred procedure was to remove tartar from the teeth by washing them with the finger, using castile soap.

A few drops of tincture of myrrh were suggested as the basis for a mouth wash. Ladies were told that the dyeing of eyelids was both foolish and vulgar and that they should shun cosmetics and washes for the skin, lest they lose their schoolgirl complexion.

THE WEEKLY SHAVE.

AN ELECTRIC FLESH BRUSH.

A CHILDREN'S BATHING TUB.

AN ADULT'S TUB.

A WASHBASIN.

A STEAM BATH

Feminine Manners

Ladies, especially younger ones, used to operate under many more restrictions than they now do. For example, the older etiquette books stated that a young lady never appears in a public place unless with her husband or in the company of older ladies. Thus, had there been movies in those days, young ladies never would have attended in groups consisting only of their own noisy and giggling kind.

Moreover, a lady never was to appear in public after her wedding invitations were issued. Today this would mean three weeks of seclusion.

A lady always entered a carriage with her back to the seat and never sat next to her escort when in the carriage. He sat facing her. To sit next to him, especially on his left, would indicate that she was not a lady, but rather his mistress. This rule did not hold, however, when the escort was driving.

A lady never was to demand a favor or attentions of a gentleman. Presumably this meant she would never ask him for a date, a present, or a refreshment. If she wished to give a present to a man, she was advised to make it herself in the form of a painting, a drawing, or some needlework.

The ladies were told they need never recognize later any man they happened to meet at the home of a friend or a man they happened to have danced with the night before. As one authority put it, "An introduction for dancing does not give a man the right to bow in the future." A lady could cut such a casual acquaintance cold if she chose to do so.

A lady was never to look in a mirror after leaving home, and when crossing a

A LADY NEVER RAISED HER VOICE.

mudpuddle was instructed to lift her skirt with one hand only. To use two hands would be undignified. And she was never to run across the street to avoid being run over by a horse and carriage. Running was regarded as inelegant and apparently more dangerous than being hit.

Until just a few years ago, ladies wore wide-brimmed hats to the theater and kept them on throughout the performance. It was not until the males started protesting and signs reading "Ladies will please remove their hats" were flashed on the movie screen that the practice reluctantly was abandoned.

Ladies were told that it was out of place to take a party of debutantes to a cabaret (meaning night club), and that a lady need not offer refreshments to callers in the city. When dining out in a restaurant attached to a saloon, ladies were urged to use the "Ladies Entrance" instead of the main one.

There was a time when women even accepted the belief that a woman's place was in the home (except for church, shops, and the theater), that a lady went into confinement for some weeks before giving birth, and that children should be seen but not heard.

Ladies were told that members of a family should not converse together in society and that married couples should not play cards together or dance with one another at a ball or cotillion.

At one time, it also was held that a lady never crossed her legs, placed her hands on her hips, or twisted sideways or leaned back in a chair. Ladies were told also that they should avoid exposing their arms and neck at a dinner party by wearing a lace or muslin overwaist.

And a lady was never to offer her hand when introduced, except in great intimacy, meaning presumably when introduced to someone she already knew very well.

LADY GODIVA FORGETS HER MANNERS.

Masculine Manners

The old etiquette books also contained a good deal of advice for men. At an evening party, for example, men were cautioned never to spend their time talking to other men. Instead, they should give their full attention to the ladies, but should avoid politics, science, religion, sports, and business topics. Since gentlemen ordinarily do not talk about housework, raising children, or new recipes, the subjects for conversation were obviously quite limited.

At the same time, men were told they never should go to an evening entertainment without their wife; that what was good enough for the men was good enough for the ladies too.

A gentlemen was cautioned not to remove his glove to shake hands with a lady, since the perspiration on his hand might ruin her glove. Nor was he to stand holding her parasol while she searched through her wristbag (purse) for keys or other objects.

When taking a lady for a drive in a carriage, a gentleman should provide her with a fan, parasol, and shawl before taking his seat across from her. He was told always to wear gloves on the street, at every party, at the opera, at theater parties, when paying calls, and when riding or driving, but not at dinner and not when out in the country.

If a draft or other cause should make it necessary for him to keep his hat on while indoors with a lady, the gentleman was to ask her permission to do so. He should remove his hat when meeting a man of position or someone he wished to conciliate. When greeting a lady or a man to be impressed, the gentleman should raise his hat twenty degrees from his head. It was correct to bow from the waist when greeting a lady or other acquaintance, and any bow should be returned.

When traveling, a gentleman always should be armed with a knife or gun and should remove his boots before getting into bed. It was taken for granted that every gentleman would know how to fence, box, ride, swim, and shoot.

Finally, the gentleman was advised never to grab anyone by the buttonhole as a means of forcing him to listen and never to insult a lady by smiling in her presence on the street. He was told that the kiss of respect is on the hand, the kiss of affection is on the cheek or forehead; only the kiss of love or passion is on the mouth.

In those early, class-conscious days, a gentleman was told never to present an inferior to a superior of the same sex. Instead, you introduced the superior to the inferior, or else made no introduction.

Finally, it was urged that any gentleman whose face was not completely covered by a beard would shave, or have himself shaved, at least once a week and, for that purpose, many men kept a shaving mug of their own in a rack at the local barber shop.

SOME MEN RAISE THEIR HAT.

OTHER MEN REMOVE THEIR HAT.

NOT ONE GENTLEMAN IN THE CAR.

A MAN IS KING OF HIS CASTLE.

So far as outer garments are concerned, the tendency in the old days was to wear more at both ends. Necklines, hemlines, and waistlines did not fluctuate like the tides as they tend to do today. For many years prior to the advent of the short skirt, women wore skirts that not only reached but swept the ground. Among their accessories were lorgnettes, muffs, and fans.

In the days when all ladies carried fans in warm weather, younger ladies used their fans to practice a form of silent communication with beaux and suitors, or perhaps personable strangers, known as fan language. It was designed both to transmit personal messages to males and to engage in silent flirtation without attracting the attention of chaperones or other observers.

Kissing the end of a fan, and simultaneously directing a loving glance at a suitor, meant "Yes, I love you."

Tapping the forehead slightly with the fan meant "I need time to think over our love."

Feminine Attire

The really significant changes that have taken place in feminine attire through the years are not in design and style but rather in quantity, complexity, and material. The wholesomely clad Gibson Girl, the boyish flapper, and more recently the quickly discarded New Look come and go.

It is generally agreed that, in early days, men and women both dressed very simply in skins and nothing else. The temperature presumably determined how many skins were worn. Then, as feminine delicacy and modesty came to the fore, the number of garments worn multiplied rapidly and their mass also increased.

A GROUP OF SCHOOL GIRLS.

A quick stroke to the chin with a closed fan told a man, "How handsome you are."

Striking a closed fan against the palm of the hand, while peering about, meant "Be careful, Mamma may be watching us."

Rubbing the nose with a fan expressed a doubt or a suggestion that a suitor had been a bit mischievous.

Moving an open fan the way birds move their wings while flying meant that the lady's beloved was far away and that she was sending her love.

Moving an open fan rapidly, accom-

YOUNG MARRIED LADIES.

panied by a dirty look, told a man, "You are a pain in the neck."

In the days before we had ready-made clothing stores, department stores, and specialty shops—all of them comparatively recent developments—milady either made her own clothes, got her mother or another relative to make them, or else retained the services of a skilled dressmaker who made them to measure in the home.

A greater variety of dress materials was used—more velvet, rich laces, satin, plush, gauze, nankeen, damask, and brocade—than is used today. Quite *de rigueur* were the high-boned collar, the leg-o'mutton sleeve, and the peekaboo waist.

As for dressing for a formal ball, it was stated that "the richest velvets, the

A SMALL WAIST.

A MEANS TO A SMALL WAIST.

A LORGNETTE.

A DRESS THAT SWEPT THE PAVEMENT.

brightest and most delicate tints in silk, elaborate coiffeurs, a large display of diamonds, artificial flowers for the head-dress and natural flowers for the hand bouquet, all belong, more or less, to the costume for a large ball." Ladies were advised to check their dress colors by both natural light and gaslight, since there was no electricity.

"The material for a dress for a drive through the public streets of a city or along a fashionable drive or park cannot be too rich. Silks, velvets and laces all are appropriate with rich jewelry and costly furs in cold weather. If fashion requires it, the carriage dress may be long enough to trail. A jacket of velvet or a shawl or a fur-trimmed mantle are the concomitants of the carriage dress for winter," as one authority put it.

For morning calls, always made after noon, the dress "should be of silk with collars and cuffs of the finest lace, light gloves, a full dress bonnet and a jewelry of gold, either burnished or enameled, or of cameo or coral."

For the promenade, the jewelry worn should be "bracelets, cuff buttons, plain gold earrings, and a gold watch chain and broach." The approved riding habit "should fit perfectly without being tight. The skirt must be full and long enough to cover the feet but not of extreme length." The hobble skirt did not come along until after the end of the nineteenth century.

A young dinner hostess was advised to wear a dress of rich silk, black or dark in color, with collar and cuffs of fine lace, and, if the dinner be by daylight, plain jewelry, but by gaslight, diamonds."

It is in the realm of innerwear or lingerie, however, that the major changes have taken place in feminine attire. Although the typical female of today owns only about five different kinds of underwear, she wore none at all in the early days, and then adopted the shift, a sort of slip, made of cotton or linsey-woolsey. From that simple start she went on to develop an impressive and diversified list, reaching the point where, around

A PARASOL.

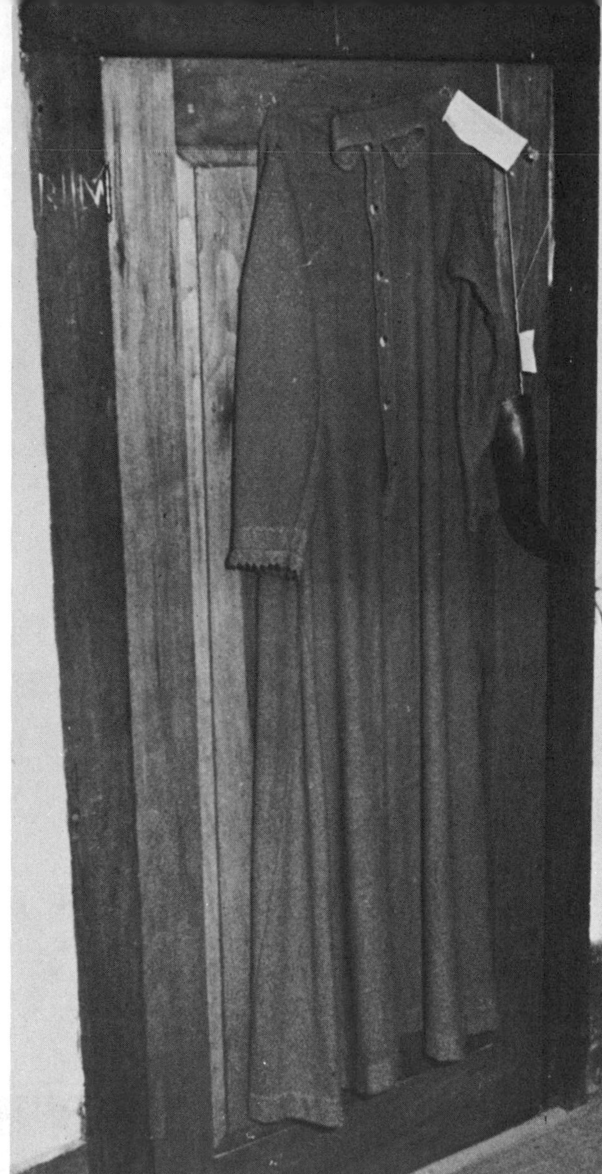

A RED FLANNEL NIGHTGOWN.

the end of the nineteenth century, the well-dressed female had not only the slip and petticoat still worn on occasion today, but also her corsets or stays; her drawers—long and medium long—and her pantalettes and bloomers; her bustles, known also as tournures and bishops; her chemises and smocks, and her chemisettes, corset covers, tuckers, camisoles, undervests, underwaists, and undershirts. Later, for a brief period, she also had her combinations or teddies. While she did not wear all these undergarments at one time, she never appeared publicly in anything like the small handful worn today.

The long flannel nightgown, complete with nightcap, was standard for bedwear in winter, giving way to a cotton gown known as a night-rail in summertime. For working or loafing about the home, milady wore her silk or flannel wrapper, her kimono, and her Mother Hubbard in place of the housecoat or shirt and shorts she favors today. A dustcap also was worn when cleaning was done via the broom instead of the vacuum cleaner.

A MAIDEN AND HER MUFF.

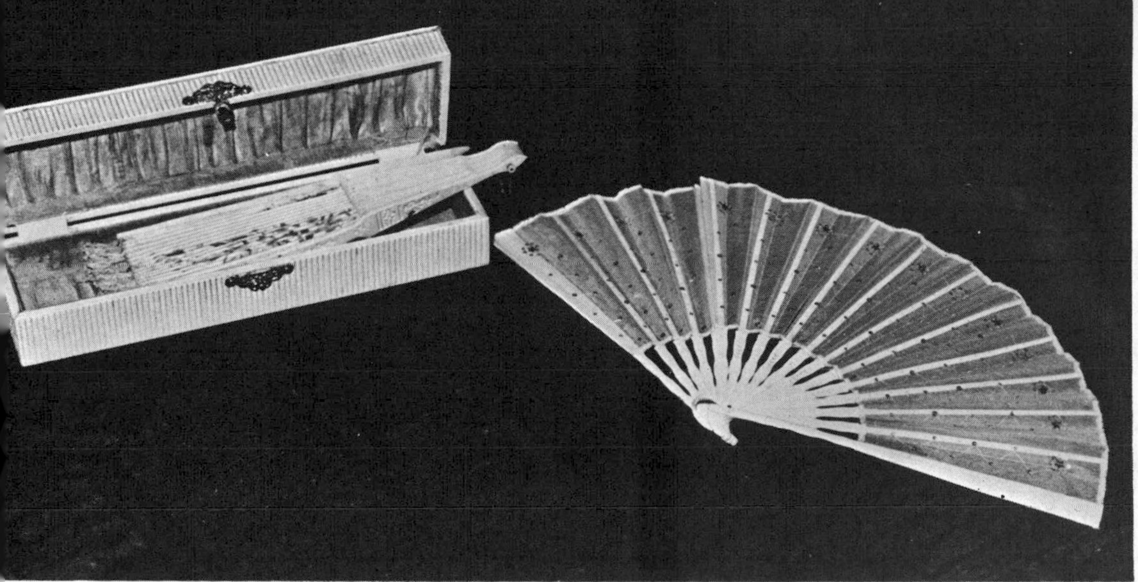

MILADY'S FAN.

For special purposes the lady of the nineteenth century had special garments, like the ingenious Angel Drawers recommended for travel abroad by one anonymous authority on decorum who later turned out to be a man. Angel Drawers were introduced and described as follows:

> [Angel drawers] are made of linen or cotton and consist of a waist cut like a plain corset cover but extending all in a piece in front with the drawers which button on the side. Usually the waists of these drawers are made without sleeves or with only a short cap at the top of the arm but for a European trip it is advisable to add sleeves to the waist, so that cuffs—paper cuffs, if preferred—can be buttoned to them.
>
> Then, in one garment, easily removed and as easily washed as a chemise, is comprised drawers, chemise, corset cover, and undersleeves, the whole taking up no more room than a single article of underwear and saving the trouble attending the care and putting on of many pieces. A gauze flannel vest underneath is perhaps a necessary precaution, and ladies who wear corsets can place them next to them. Over there the single garment adds all that is required in the way of underwear, except two skirts and a small light hair-cloth tornure.

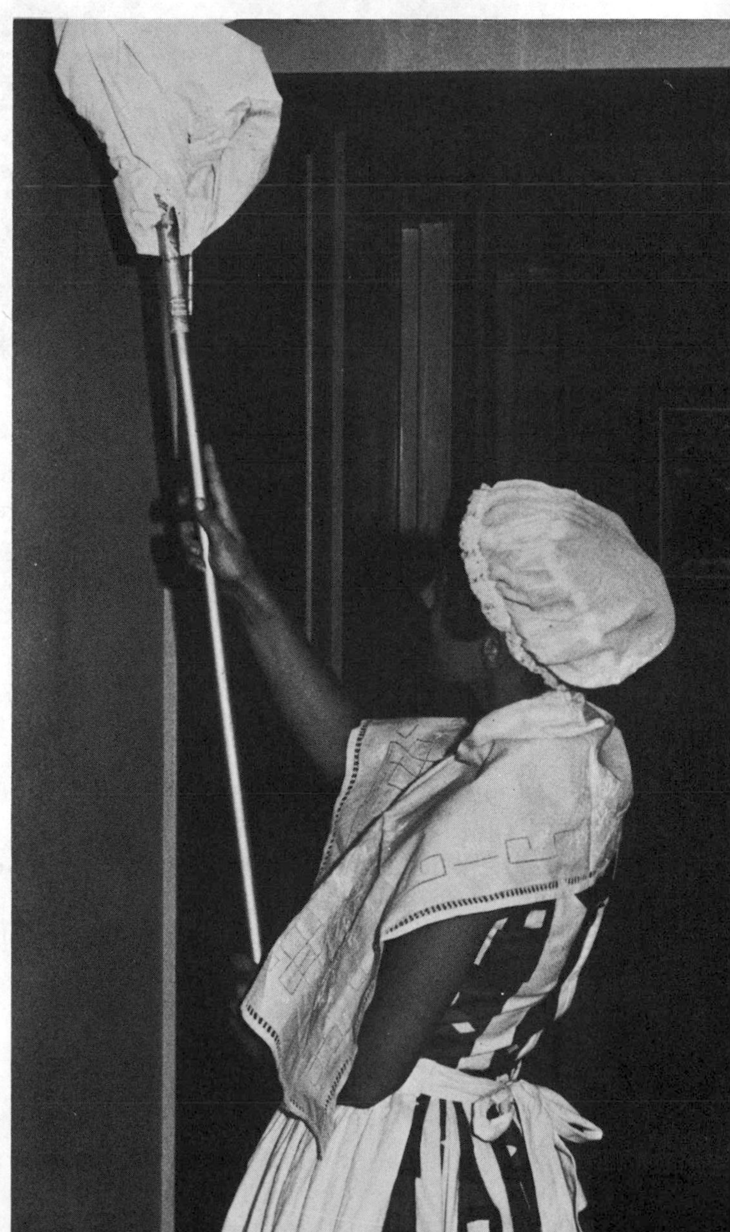

A DUST CAP.

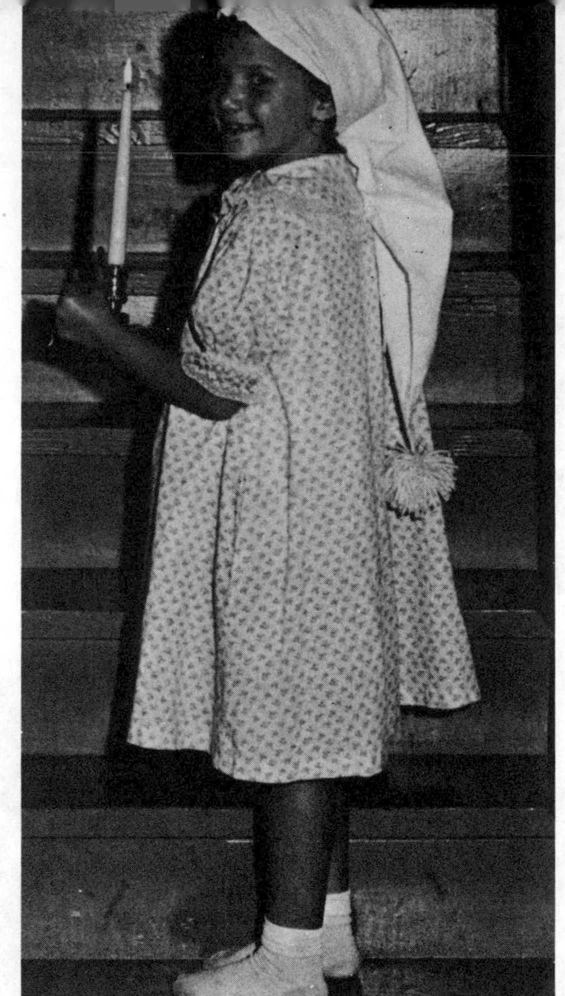

A NIGHTCAP.

When traveling anywhere, ladies were advised to carry a satchel with a change of collars, cuffs, and gloves. Money could be carried in the bosom. They also were advised to carry a waterproof shawl with shawl straps in case of rain.

Sturdy shoes were the rule in the days when streets were full of mud. One authority said women's shoes should have a broad sole and a half-inch heel as broad at the bottom as at the top.

There were variations, of course. The wardrobe provided for a school girl in colonial Virginia was reported as consisting of:

A cap, ruffle and tucker
1 pair white stays
2 pairs white kid gloves
2 pairs colored kid gloves
3 pairs thread hose
1 pair silk shoes laced
1 pair Morocco shoes
1 hoop coat
1 hat
4 pairs plain Spanish shoes
2 pairs calf Spanish shoes
1 mask
1 fan
1 necklace
1 girdle (belt) and buckle
1 piece fashionable calico
1½ yards of cambric
4 yards of ribbon
A mantua and coat

Dresses and underwear, if any, presumably were taken for granted.

YOUTHFUL ENVY.

A WOMAN'S CROWNING GLORY.

WOODEN SHOES.

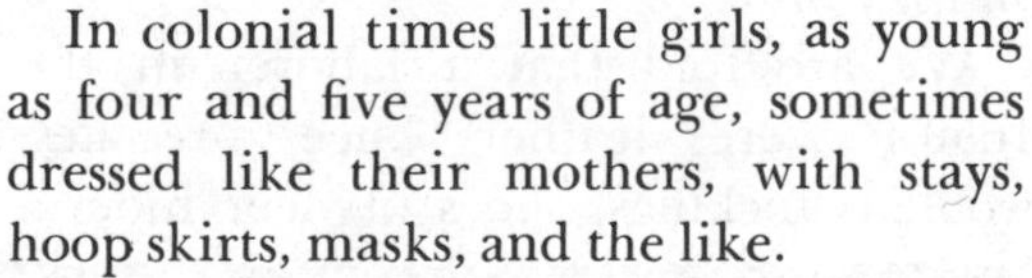

In colonial times little girls, as young as four and five years of age, sometimes dressed like their mothers, with stays, hoop skirts, masks, and the like.

Shawls, mantuas, and dolmans were standard equipment for milady before she started going everywhere in an automobile. Her favorite overgarment was the cloak, known also as a roquelaure, capuchin, or pelisse.

Until the daring era of bobbed hair came along, most ladies wore their hair full-length, although they usually did it up in waterfalls, in buns, piled high on the head, or braided to keep the tresses under control. Hair long enough to sit on was not at all uncommon. Ladies often had to sleep sitting up in a chair to keep from spoiling fancy new hair-dos arranged well ahead of time for a big ball by an overly popular hairdresser.

Beauty parlors were unknown in those days, and milady took care of her own hair, except on special occasions, unless she was fortunate enough to have a lady's maid in her employ. Hair was curled with the aid of iron curlers heated over the stove, rags, rolls of paper, and pieces of kid.

Along with her long hair, every lady

A YOUNG GIRL'S DRESS.

owned a variety of accessories such as shell hairpins and hatpins. To change or improve the shape of her hair-do, she used rats, switches, and chignons and often adorned her hair with a colorful hair ribbon. Spit curls and bangs were even more common than today. Ear lobes were pierced to accommodate the earrings of the day.

To protect her peaches-and-cream complexion from the dangerous rays of the sun, milady wore sunbonnets, broad-brimmed hats, masks, and veils, and then carried a parasol in the bargain. The wife of an early U. S. President was described as wearing a mask of linen, long-armed gloves, and a sunbonnet, sewed on, to protect her from the burning sun. Sunburn and tanned skin were regarded as a blemish.

Some ladies owned a wide variety of hats, most of them large and broad, but the more thrifty girl got by on one basic straw or felt hat for the year around, changing the trimming as each new season arrived: an ostrich feather in winter, fresh flowers in summer, and so on.

Masculine Attire

The changes in men's fashions which take place today are mild, indeed, compared to the sweeping changes that have occurred since colonial days. Leather, widely worn in early times, is seen today only in sports apparel, and homespun is gone forever.

Color was rampant in 1770. An advertisement offered men's woolens in scarlet, buff, blue, green, crimson, white, and sky blue.

We are told that a laborer in the 1650's wore leather knee breeches, woolen stockings, shoes of deer hide, a

A STIFF COLLAR.

CARRYING A CANE.

SILVER SHOE BUCKLES.

leather coat with pewter buttons, a shirt of coarse gray cloth, and a rabbit cap with the fur still on. It will be noted again that there is no mention of underwear, which was worn sparingly in those days.

A typical New England laborer some years later wore a rough suit of canvas, buckskin, or leather with pewter buttons, cotton stockings, shoes with wooden heels, and a monmouth cap.

The Massachusetts Bay Company furnished each of its men with four pairs of shoes, four pairs of stockings, one pair of garters, two suits or doublets and hose of leather lined with oiled skin, one woolen suit lined with leather, one green cotton waistcoat, one leather belt, one black hat, two red knit caps, two pairs of gloves, one cotton-lined cloak, one extra pair of breeches, two handkerchiefs, and four bands or collars. Again underwear is not mentioned.

The attire of a prosperous colonial, on the other hand, is described as consisting of a waistcoat of scarlet velvet, broadcloth or silk, knee breeches, a dark brown coat of fustian with silver buttons and large pockets flared out almost to the knees, a white linen shirt and collar, and a felt hat with a wide brim, high crown, and plume.

John Hancock at the time of the revolution was reported to have worn a scarlet velvet cap, a blue damask gown lined with velvet, a white satin embroidered waistcoat, black satin small clothes (trousers), white silk stockings, and red morocco slippers.

A few years later, a Boston printer appeared wearing a pea-green coat, white vest, nankeen (brownish-yellow) small clothes, white silk stockings, and pumps

WEARING HAND-ME-DOWNS.

A MONOCLE.

fastened with huge silver buckles. His small clothes were tied at the knees with ribbons of the same color in double bows, the ends reaching nearly to the ankles.

A Virginia colonel in the 1700's wore a blue dress coat with brass buttons, light colored pantaloons, a black satin vest, dark silk cravat, and a broad-brimmed felt hat. A gentleman of the same State wore a broadcloth coat with silver buttons, sleeves edged with ruffles and cuffs, a colored waistcoat ornamented with turkey work, olive colored plush or broadcloth breeches, silk stockings, shoes with silver buckles, deerskin gloves, and a silk mantle or scarlet cloak.

On the other hand, a Broadway fop or dandy favored patent leather boots, wide striped pants which were tight except around the boots, watch chain and seal, heavy finger ring, fancy cravat of broad-tail style, standing shirt collar, sack coat of fancy suede just covering his hips, with sleeves large and loose over the hand, full beard, quizzing glass or monocle over the left eye, hair befrizzled to the utmost, a short walking stick under his arm, white hat on the left side of his head, and gray leather gloves.

Beards and other facial hair were commonplace in the early days when men were outdoors long hours in the cold and when shaving was far less convenient than it is today. Among the favored styles were the goatee, mutton chop, sidewhiskers, burnsides, dundrearies, and the Galway slugger.

Wigs also had their day, except among the Puritans who wore their hair long in back and tied in a queue or pigtail. Wigs, which sometimes reached almost to the waist, were made of various kinds of hair—human, horse, goat, and calf, including cow tails. A wig with a queue was called a false-tail. There were tie wigs, bag wigs, nightcap wigs, bob wigs, and riding wigs, among others. On special occasions, some men also carried muffs, made of fox or other fur.

Winter coats were made of buffalo hide and raccoon. Pants or breeches were commonly made of buckskin, deerskin, and rawhide. Caps were made from beaver, coonskin, foxskin, and rabbit. Hats worn by men have ranged from the rabbit and beaver to the tricorn or three-cornered cocked hat, the slouch hat with both wide and narrow brim, the derby, and the homburg.

A BOILED SHIRT.

The woolen and red-flannel underwear with long arms and legs is still worn today only by a handful of men who work outdoors and by some older people who fear the cold. The union suit, which combined undershirt and pants, now is a curiosity, and the old-fashioned long night shirt has given way to pajamas.

Before the comfortable soft collar came along, city men of any distinction whatsoever wore detachable stiff collars, made of rubber or paper or else starched linen. Some of those old collars were pretty high and could get quite uncomfortable, but they were in style. They were worn with a shirt that had a collar band, requiring one collar button in front and another behind to keep the collar in place. The wearing of stiff collars declined gradually but steadily into

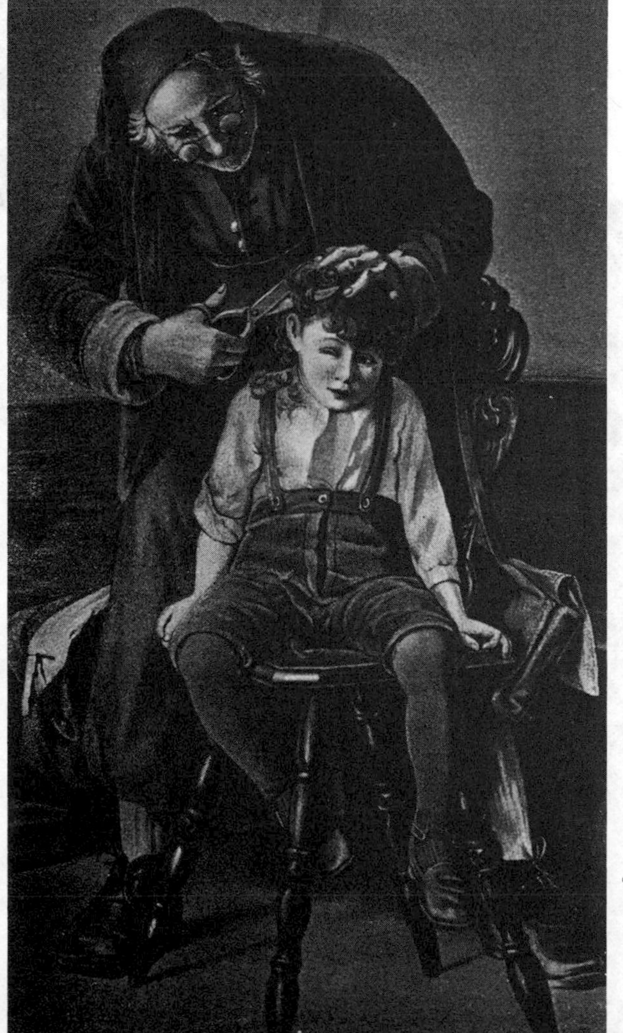

THE CURLS MUST GO.

the twentieth century, finally being limited to use with formal attire and by clergymen. Ex-President Herbert Hoover wore one of the highest on record and was one of the last men in public life to cling to his stiff collar.

Shirts worn with stiff collars had either detachable or attached cuffs which also were starched and required the wearing of cuff links, as do some shirts today. Dressier shirts also had starched bosoms. Most suits had vests and some had pegtop trousers. High shoes were the rule until just a few decades back.

The auto heater has made earmuffs, foot warmers, and laprobes superfluous. Among men, knee buckles, shoe buckles, spats, and ruffles are things of the past. Dickies, sleeve garters, reversible collars, celluloid collars, paper collars, rubber collars, and detachable cuffs are seen no more. The same is largely true of the once popular cane or walking stick, stickpin, watch chain and fob, and various other accessories once considered indispensable to the well-dressed man.

A LONG MOUSTACHE.

AN OLD-FASHIONED NIGHTSHIRT.

HIS FIRST STORE-BOUGHT SUIT.

The young boy now progresses directly from diapers to shorts to long trousers. Long forgotten are the knee-length pants with the buckles, the Peter Thompson suits, the Buster Brown collars, and other garments that most boys always rejected as being entirely too feminine.

Most boys, and their sisters too, wore hand-me-downs, which might have been worn by several older members of the family. Well-made clothes somehow lasted for generations in those days. Getting a brand new suit, let alone a store-bought one, was a great occasion for a nineteenth century youngster—an experience some youths never enjoyed.

WORKING ATTIRE.

Sports Attire

Because of their innate modesty women were slow to adopt sports attire and played all manner of games in long, full skirts that seldom revealed an ankle and sometimes swept the ground, although for croquet, archery, and skating, one fashion authority of the late 1880's advocated a "short skirt displaying a handsomely fitted, but stout, boot."

With the voluminous skirts were worn long-sleeved, high-necked shirt-waists and small-waisted jackets that obiously required tight corsets. Women's sleeves usually were long whether the sport was tennis, bowls, horseback riding, ice skating, snow-shoeing, badminton, croquet, row-boating, canoeing, sailboating, yachting, or golf.

The authority added that "the hat should have a broad brim so as to shield the face from the sun and render a parasol unnecessary." The straw boater was favored for sailing and various other sports.

Only in gymnastics, ordinarily practiced in the privacy of a gymnasium from which male spectators were barred, did the young ladies shed their skirts in favor of bloomers and even then they wore high-necked, long-sleeved blouses and long stockings.

Society games, such as indoor badminton, sometimes were played by both sexes in formal attire.

Later on, as women began to compete more seriously in golf and tennis, skirts were shortened, half-sleeves began to appear, and necklines dropped a bit, but the fashionable society golfer of the feminine sex still might appear in a starched collar and tie and a broad-brimmed hat.

Male sportsmen quickly adopted the tight, short knicker with long stockings for all of the more vigorous sports—football, bicycling, hare-and-hounds, distance and cross-country running, lacrosse, baseball, etc. They usually wore hats or caps and for the most part long sleeves. Later, for tennis, the colorful blazer and white flannels became standard equipment, with cap, tie, and blazer all matching.

CURLERS.

Numerous changes have been made in football attire. The turtle-necked jersey and the canvas vest have disappeared, while the headguard has replaced the long hair worn to protect the head from injury. The awkward rubber nose-guard has been replaced by a special protector attached to the headguard. Elbow pads and shin guards are unknown today, unless a player has an injury to be protected at those points.

While volunteer fire fighting was a serious matter, it also had its sporting aspects in the early days when men of substance belonged to the fire companies and would turn out for a fire in high beaver hats, frilled shirt fronts, and long-tailed coats, plus high rubber boots.

A FEMININE ARCHER.

PLAYING THE STONES.

ARCHERS.

SKATING A DEUX

FIGURE SKATING.

ICE-SKATING.

THREE'S A CROWD.

SNOWSHOEING.

TOBOGGANING.

ROLLER SKATING.

CROQUET PLAYERS.

BICYCLING.

TAKING PHYSICAL CULTURE.

BOWLING.

LADY GYMNASTS.

RIDING SIDE-SADDLE.

RIDING IN THE PARK.

BATTLEDORE AND SHUTTLECOCK.

FORMAL BADMINTON.

TENNIS IN THE PARK.

TENNIS BY THE SEA.

MALE TENNIS PLAYERS.

BOWLING ON THE GREEN.

YACHTING.

CRUISING.

BOATING.

SAILING.

MEMBERS OF THE CREW.

FISHING.

FOOT RACERS.

PLAYING HARE AND HOUNDS.

CROSS-COUNTRY RUNNERS.

POLO PLAYERS.

PLAYING LACROSSE.

A FOOTBALL GAME.

"DOWN"

INJURY ON THE FIELD.

PLAYING CRICKET.

SAFE AT HOME.

A GENTLEMAN DRESSED FOR SHOOTING.

HUNTERS IN INFORMAL GARB.

INFORMAL GOLF ATTIRE.

THE STYLISH LADY GOLFER.

GOLFERS IN KNICKERS.

Medicine

The practice of medicine has come a long way since it was in the hands of the medical faker, the barber-surgeon-dentist, and the preacher-physician. No longer do our physicians bleed or leech their patients, and we have ceased quarantining children in their homes, with warning signs on the door, for childhood diseases such as measles and mumps. Hospitals have taken the place of pest houses, and our social service agencies have made poor farms and poorhouses unnecessary.

Our dentists now do not place the patient's head between their knees when extracting teeth, nor do they use a "cant hook" in doing so. Moreover, they have discontinued the practice of replacing extracted human teeth with the teeth of sheep and other animals.

AN EMERGENCY INNOCULATION.

On the advice of the modern physician, we no longer compel our young and ailing relatives to down a spring tonic consisting of sulphur and molasses, nor do we prescribe sassafras tea or a blood purifier consisting of burdock root, sasca root, dandelion root, and hops.

In the old days, herb tea, including that made from catnip, was prescribed for colds, and a brew made from bitter southernwood was fed to love-sick maidens.

We no longer believe that ague is caused by exposure to heavy dews, thus requiring us to close our bedroom windows at night.

In addition, we have abandoned the customs of putting garlic in our shoes to prevent fever, going bathing in the sea to prevent or relieve gout, dropping roasted hedgehog fat in the ear to relieve deafness, wearing a fawn's-tooth necklace to promote early teething, and shaving off a beard to cure baldness. We no longer wear liver pads or electric belts to cure back aches.

We have learned that there is, after all, no danger in eating certain food combinations such as fish and ice cream, or cucumbers and ice cream, and we now know that fish does not excel as brain food.

The physician, in the early days, visited his patients via horseback or horse and buggy, and babies were delivered at home on the kitchen table.

Before there was a drugstore on almost every corner and a host of patent medicines or proprietary preparations for every known ailment, the physician or patient had to concoct or mix his own, and cookbooks and other publications presented formulas for doing so. Thus, to make healing salve, one would "heat in an earthen dish one pound of leaf lard, one pound of mutton tallow, five cents worth of yellow beeswax, and five cents worth of raw linseed oil," to which, when cold, one added a large handful of elder bark obtained by scraping off the gray and using only the green of the bark. This then was "set on the fire and boiled for 20 minutes, strained through a cloth, and stirred until cold." It was to be made in the spring.

Cough syrup could be made by "combining one pound of loaf sugar, one-half pound of flax seed, four sliced lemons, and two quarts of water; boil and strain; add one pint of whiskey or brandy to preserve."

As a wash for inflamed feet, one combined "one ounce of spirits of camphor, one ounce of ammonia, and one coffee cup of ocean salt. Put in a quart bottle, fill with water, shake well, and then add three or four teaspoons to a bowl of water."

In this connection, one early cookbook recommended that "Persons with dyspepsia or troubled with slow digestion will find it to their advantage to avoid combinations such as fruit and vegetables; milk and vegetables; sugar and milk, meat, or vegetables; fats with fruits, meat, vegetables."

Another cookbook stated that "use of condiments is unquestionably a strong auxiliary to a formation of a habit of using intoxicating beverages. False appetite aroused by use of food that burns and stings craves something less insipid than pure cold water to keep up the fever the food has excited. Condiments, like all other stimulants, must be continually increased in quantity or their effect becomes diminished, and this leads to a demand for stronger stimulants, both in eating and drinking, until the probable tendency is toward the dram shop."

The fad of going to a favorite spa or watering place to "take the waters" for what ailed you has greatly declined, although some of the spas retain their popularity as resorts.

Use of Tobacco

It was not so many years back that cigarette smokers were looked on both as sissies and as candidates for an early demise. Devotees of cigars and other stronger forms of the weed scorned the softies who used cigarettes, which were popularly known as coffin nails. Women, of course, never touched the things in those days.

A DOCTOR ON HORSEBACK.

A FANCY CUSPIDOR.

In the absence of today's cigarettes, the he-men of the earlier era smoked cigars, chewed chawin' tobacco, and dipped snuff. The smaller the man—or boy—the larger the cigar; that was the rule, or so it seemed. Cigar smokers once were so plentiful that children and girls saved cigar bands—the colorful paper rings that run about the middle of a cigar showing the brand name—and pasted them on the bottom of glass dishes where they would show through from beneath. Girls vied with one another to see who had the largest number of different kinds of cigar bands.

A cheaper way to enjoy tobacco was to chew it, and this was the practice where smoking was dangerous or forbidden as in mines, barns, factories, and homes where the housewife would not tolerate the heavy smoke of cigars in her draperies. To accommodate cigar butts and ashes and the expectoration that accompanies tobacco chewing, it became necessary to install spittoons or cuspidors in all inside public places and in many homes. These receptacles assumed various forms and shapes but eventually were banished from the home by the outraged and persistent womenfolk. Chewing still persists where smoking is inconvenient or forbidden.

Snuff, too, was used mainly where smoking was discouraged. It was taken up by sophisticates of both sexes in the upper echelons of society, and a snuffbox was standard equipment in many boudoirs, where silver snuffboxes were especially treasured belongings. The powdery tobacco product was consumed either by inhaling it through a nostril or else by rubbing it on the gums with a finger.

The etiquette books of the latter part of the nineteenth century devoted considerable space to cigar smoking in view of the then prominent part it played in social life. Men were told, for example,

A COMMON SPITTOON.

INTRODUCING BABY TO SNUFF.

that a gentleman never keeps a cigar in his mouth when talking to or saluting a lady on the street and never spits in the presence of a lady.

The males were advised also that they should never smoke in the presence of a lady without asking permission and, indeed, never should go in the presence of a lady with tobacco on their breath. In addition, a gentleman should never smoke in a room that ladies frequent, "since few ladies like the odor of tobacco in their clothes." Chewing parsley was recommended to remove the odor and taste of a cigar.

The practice of spitting, as practiced by cigar smokers and tobacco chewers, was considered offensive by many people, especially women of delicate sensibilities. One feminine visitor from

SHARING SNUFF WITH THE CROWD.

Europe wrote in her journal that the "incessant, contaminating, remorseless, loathesome spitting by American men" was one of the great drawbacks of her trip.

Further back, in colonial days, the use of tobacco was placed under strict regulation in some places, even though the raw product was acceptable in payment of fines, taxes, and lodging, and as a dowry. In some places, for example, no one could use tobacco publicly, no two men could smoke together, and no one could smoke within two miles of the meeting-house on the Sabbath. Landlords were forbidden to permit tobacco to be taken into their houses on penalty of a fine for both landlord and tobacco user.

The Puritans presumably frowned on tobacco because it gave pleasure to the user but others feared its effect on the health of the smoker, leading to such regulations as "No person under twenty-one shall take any tobacco until someone skilled in physics testifies that it is useful to him and he has received a license from the court."

Folklore

The folklore of our grandfathers included many quaint beliefs and superstitions, few of which remain today. Some of the more popular superstitions had to do with animal life, such as:

A hog should be slaughtered in the light of the moon.

Feeding gunpowder to dogs will make them fierce.

A snake can't die until sundown.

A mare's milk is good for toothache.

If a rooster crows or a dog or fox barks near a sick room, death is near.

In addition to accepting such symbols of bad luck as black cats and walking under ladders, our forefathers were sure it was bad luck to:

Let a tree or a third person come between two individuals.

Shake hands across a gate.

Sweep the floor after sunset.

Get married in May.

Begin a job on Friday.

Let a woman sing before breakfast.

Open an umbrella in the house.

Rock an empty chair.

Spill salt on the table.

Get out of bed on a different side than you got in on.

Drop a piece of bread with the buttered side up.

Light three cigarettes on one match.

Let a bride see the groom before the

A HORSESHOE OVER THE DOOR.

wedding on her wedding day.

Let the bride walk across the threshold of her new home after the wedding.

Let a bride look into a mirror after she is dressed for the wedding.

Let a bride sew on her own wedding dress.

Step out of the house on the left foot.

Get married on Friday.

Turn back from a journey or look back at one's house after starting on a journey. (If one did return, the only way to avert bad luck was to sit down before starting out again.)

Break a mirror.

On the other hand, there also were some ways to promote good luck, such as:

Walking three times around your chair at a card game.

Accidentally putting a piece of clothing on wrongside out and then wearing it that way all day.

Having a horseshoe over the door.

Finding a horseshoe in the road.

Rubbing the hump of a hunchback.

Carrying a rabbit's foot.

Rubbing a negro's head.

Wearing of orange blossoms by a bride.

In addition, it was believed to be lucky to find something of value, to find a four-leaf clover, or to carry a lucky bone from the head of a codfish. Various talismans or charms were taken most seriously. For example, it was believed that:

Amber beads reduce goiter.

Gold beads will cure a sore throat.

Red beads are good for a nosebleed.

Cobwebs will stop bleeding.

A leather necklace guards against whooping cough.

A black cord around the neck averts croup or diptheria.

Buzzard feathers in the hatband will ward off rheumatism.

A hog's tooth in the righthand pants pocket will prevent toothache.

Many old timers were convinced that:

Rheumatism can be cured by carrying a potato in the pocket and can be prevented by carrying a horse chestnut or by wearing an eelskin or a red string around the neck.

Warts can be eliminated by rubbing them with a bean, a snail, sassafras, or raw meat, by rubbing them with milkweed which then should be buried, by rubbing them with a kernel of corn which then should be thrown to a chicken, or by rubbing them with a stolen dishcloth which then should be buried.

The itch can be prevented or cured by carrying a piece of brimstone or a small bag of sulphur.

Poison ivy can be warded off forever by eating some of it.

Cramps can be prevented by wearing an eelskin around the ankle.

Insomnia can be prevented by smelling one of the socks you have been wearing before retiring.

A sore throat can be cured by wearing one of your socks around your neck with the sole at your throat.

Tobacco juice is good for bee stings.

Whiskey is good for snake bites.

In addition, there were numerous other beliefs, such as:

If a woman whistles before breakfast, she will cry before night.

Thunder in February means frost in May.

Cold hands mean warm heart.

Watch a caller out of sight and he'll never return.

To grow good pepper, get mad when planting it.

If you spit over your left shoulder and make a wish when you see the first star at night, the wish will come true.

A dream told before breakfast will come true.

A pregnant woman should be fed everything she asks for.

Catastrophes come in threes.

If your ears burn, someone is talking about you.

If your nose itches, you are being vexed by a fool or you are going to have a quarrel.

Lightning never strikes the same place twice.

2. Our Everyday Activities

Woman's Work

Whatever the facts may be today, few American women were pampered prior to the latter part of the nineteenth century. Whether they lived on farms as many did, or in towns and villages, the woman kept physically busy from dawn to dusk and later, as did their husbands and older children. There was precious little time for PTA meetings, women's or garden clubs, voters' or planned parenthood meetings, and other feminine organizations such as we know today. Indeed, young girls were so busy with urgent family work that they had all too little time to spend on formal education.

One farm wife in Ohio told a visitor her farm was so self-sufficient that she needed money only to buy coffee, tea, and whisky. She said she could raise whatever money she needed any day by sending butter and chickens to market. Except for iron to make implements and some salt, everything the family really required was raised or made on the farm.

The farmer's lady played an important part in filling those needs. To provide clothing for the family, she and her older daughters, and perhaps grandma, carded the wool, hatcheled the flax, spun the yarn, wove the cloth, and then sewed the homespun garments that family members wore, including those made from deerskin, rawhide, and other kinds of leather. This, however, was mostly spare-time work, performed in the evening when other household work had been completed, such as washing the family clothes aided by a large tub and washboard and ironing them with flatirons that had to be heated on the top of the stove.

Naturally, the farmwife also cooked the food, baked the bread, pies, biscuits, and cakes, and put up the jellies, jams, and preserves in her kingsized kitchen with its huge open fireplace and later its iron range. There was no store-bought bread or jam in those days and, if there had been, the family would not have had the money to buy them.

THE WHOLE FAMILY WORKING.

The good lady also made or helped make essential household supplies by churning butter, pouring candles, pickling and salting meat, and making soap out of grease and leached ashes.

Those were the indoor activities. Out in the barnyard and environs, she milked cows, fed chickens and pigs, picked fruits and berries, and assisted in rendering lard. She helped to sow the fields at planting time and then helped with the harvest by raking hay, gleaning the grain, and driving the horses that pulled the farm equipment.

In later years when the tractor or separator came to harvest the grain, the farm wife served a bounteous repast at noon to the ravenous farm hands and neighboring farmers who came to help get in the crop. In between other duties, she planted and operated the farm garden, served as a shepherdess, and helped nurse the sick horse or cow. On occasion she often had to split and carry in wood for the stove and pump a few dozen pails of water.

Performing all these jobs and raising two, three, four or more babies at the same time required quite a bit of ingenuity, but Mother was up to it. She had to be. After a little experience, she found it was no trick at all to churn the butter, watch the stove, and nurse a baby at the same time.

Not until family income began to permit the hiring of "servants" was the housewife relieved of some of the multitude of duties involved in running a home.

A SPINNER AT REST.

AT REST IN THE FIELD.

Chores

In these times of store-bought food, automatic heat, and automotive transportation, life on a farm or in a town home is very different for a youngster than it was fifty or a hundred years ago. The difference consists principally of the greatly lessened number of chores to be done by young boys and girls.

Chores are defined as the regular or daily light work to be done on a farm or in a home, but some of them were none too light. On the farm, as soon as he was able to assume any responsibility, a young boy was given such jobs as going out to fetch the horses and cows in from the fields in the morning. In wintertime, the air could be mighty frosty at the beginning of the day and this chore was no cinch, but in summer the air often was clear and fresh and the only drawback to being out working was the earliness of the hour. Farm chores usually started right at or even before daybreak, especially in the planting, cultivating, and harvest seasons.

Then the various animals had to be fed their grain and hay—the horses, mules, oxen, cows, calves, sheep, pigs, chickens, ducks, geese, and other fowl. And that meant shelling and grinding corn. Someone, usually a boy or girl, also had to gather the eggs from nests in the barn, chicken house, and other odd places where the hens may have wandered.

In addition to being fed, the animals also had to be watered, which meant laboriously pumping water into troughs, tanks, and pails, unless the windmill happened to be working at the time. And when the stock had been watered, there was water to be pumped and carried into the kitchen for cooking, cleaning and washing, and the Saturday night bath. Since the used water had to be carried back out, the same way it came in—in pails—it is no wonder that water was used sparingly in those days.

GATHERING EGGS IN THE BARN.

The farm boy also was expected to help milk the cows twice a day when he became old enough, and sister joined in, too, at the proper age. When a boy was big enough, he cleaned out the stalls occupied by the cows and horses and brought in fresh straw for the animals.

When all those chores had been tended to, the male youngster turned his attention to the woodpile, where he sawed logs with his bucksaw, split them with his axe, and carried the firewood to the woodpile, the woodshed, the wood closet, or the woodbox in the kitchen next to the stove.

And if he was found with time on his hands, the farm boy was assigned to such special chores as gathering nuts, picking and paring apples, gathering berries, shelling peas, splitting shoe pegs, and collecting hog bristles. When there were no chores to be done at the moment, he could slip away for some hunting, trapping, fishing, or swimming in the old swimming hole.

MILKING OLD BETTY.

WATER GIRLS.

HELPING MOTHER EAGERLY.

Youngsters who lived in town also had their chores, some of which existed on the farm. Young girls were expected to help with carding wool, setting dye, scouring pewter, hatcheling flax, spinning thread and yarn, and weaving such items as suspenders, garters, and candlewicks, watch bands, wrist bands, and tapers. They helped clean and fill the kerosene lamps and trim the wicks, assisted in making candles, stirred batter and icing, and so on, in addition to such modern tasks as bed making, dusting, and dish washing.

Chores for the town boy consisted of shoveling coal into the furnace, shaking the grates, carrying out the ashes, beating carpets, emptying slop jars, grinding coffee, shining shoes for the family, and helping with other chores which his sister performed. There never was a dull moment, nor an idle one, if it could be helped.

HELPING GRANDMA RELUCTANTLY.

Handiwork

When there were fewer distractions than there are today and even brief idleness was regarded as a sin by right-thinking people, women (both young and old) and young children spent their spare time on handiwork, such as crocheting, embroidery, tatting, petitpoint, knitting, spatter work, and the like, mostly for home or personal use but also for gifts, for sale, or for barter. In the cities, lessons could be taken in any of those arts from special teachers.

The feminine members of the family did a great deal of knitting and turned out knitted sox and stockings, gloves and mittens, sweaters, scarfs, caps, lamp mats, and purses for the entire family, in addition to making their clothes.

The girls of the family kept busy in numerous other ways, as well, including cheese making, birch broom making, basket weaving, straw plaiting, netting fringes for edging, waxwork, lace making, and the like. Older girls engaged in filigree and feather work, painting on glass, and turkey work. They also made hair wreaths from the hair of feminine members of the family. These were framed and hung on the wall as objects of art. Samplers, embroidered with crewel or silk on linen or other firm bases, were intended to show how expert a young girl had become in her needlework and often were framed and hung on the wall.

Young children did many of these same tasks and also leaned how to hem and mark napkins, spin flax, embroider samplers and mottoes, and turn the clock-reel and swift when yarn was being wound.

Hair also was used to make bracelets, earrings, watch chains, and breast pins.

Every home had a rag bag into which were put rags or scraps of silk, linen, calico, cotton, or wool for use in quilts, rag rugs, and hooked rugs. Old underwear, sleeve linings, worn-out clothes too far

A MOTTO.

gone to be remodeled and handed down, and remnants of any kind were saved in this way.

The men folk and boys contributed by using their penknives to make toys, butter paddles, and cheese hoops, and to sharpen quills, while the more accomplished males turned out such wooden objects as piggins and noggins, runlets, keelers, firkins, buckets, churns, dye tubs, cowles, powdering tubs, hatracks, clothes trees, and picture frames. A man who made such objects professionally was known as a dish turner or wood turner.

Other items made with jackknives were gambrells for butchering, sled runners, hames for horse collars, hay hooks, bean poles and sifters, feed boxes, geese and hog yokes, thills or shafts for carts, cheese ladders, traps, flails, hoops, shingles, axe handles, mauls, singletrees and doubletrees, and door and gate latches.

All of this was over and above the major handiwork performed by the males, such as making shoes, tools, and harness. It can be seen from these lists that there was little loafing by any member of a well-regulated family. Except on special occasions, every minute had to be used productively in the early days if the family was to live any kind of a satisfying life. Yet with all these other demands, members of the family took time twice a day for devotions and Bible reading.

A HAIR WREATH.

A SAMPLER.

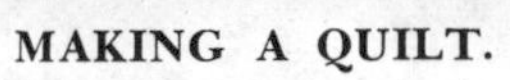

MAKING A QUILT.

WEAVING.

GRANDMA AND HER SEWING.

Religion

That the early colonists, especially the Puritans and Pilgrims, were extremely devout is obvious from the fact that they regularly sat through two- to three-hour services and sixty-minute prayers in unheated churches in the middle of winter. The small metal foot warmers some of them brought along helped a little, but the coals always burned out before the service ended.

People were summoned to church twice each Sunday and on other occasions by various methods, since few owned clocks or pocket watches. The call was given by raising a flag, ringing a bell, firing a gun or cannon, blowing a bugle or conch shell, or beating a drum.

There was a tendency to fall asleep or at least to doze off during the long services, especially in warmer weather, but that was not as easy as it sounds in pews consisting of hard plank benches with straight backs and mouldings at the top of the back to discourage slouching.

In addition, there was the tithingman, armed with a long tithing rod which had a knob on one end to awaken sleeping men and a gentler hare's foot or feather on the other to arouse the women. He also was charged with the job of keeping order among the younger children who accompanied their elders to church. If the church was large enough, there were dog pelters and dog whippers to cope with the canines who came along to help warm the feet of their masters in cold weather and were known to bay and moan during the musical intervals.

The tithingman also had the responsibility for seeing that all nearby taverns were closed during services, although the innkeepers themselves were required to clear their houses. In one place in Virginia, the Captain of the Guard searched private homes looking for church dodgers. Anyone failing to appear in church would be forcibly carried there by the tithingman or constable or a squad of soldiers.

There is a record of one individual who fell asleep so soundly and so often during services that he was fined as a "common sleeper." At least one woman

A TWO-HOUR SERMON.

READING THE SCRIPTURES.

was fined for sitting in another person's pew.

Taverns could not be closed entirely on the Sabbath because they were needed as places to rest and sources of food and liquid refreshment between services in the cold, damp churches by members of the congregation who had come some distance and had no other place to go on inclement days. Those families that brought their lunch to eat between services ate in sheds called noon-houses that had a fireplace at one end. Traffic usually was stopped in front of churches while services were in progress.

The preacher, who sometimes boarded with members of the church, just as school teachers boarded with parents of school children, frequently held another job during the week. Some of the secondary occupations on record are butcher, merchant, judge, physician, school teacher, surveyor, tavern keeper, and constable. Donation parties were held to supplement the parson's modest pay, and sewing bees were held by the good ladies of the congregation to provide garments for his family.

In the days before hymnals were generally available, it was customary for a preacher to line the hymns; that is, he would read or sing one or two lines and then the congregation would repeat them. To make sure that everyone could

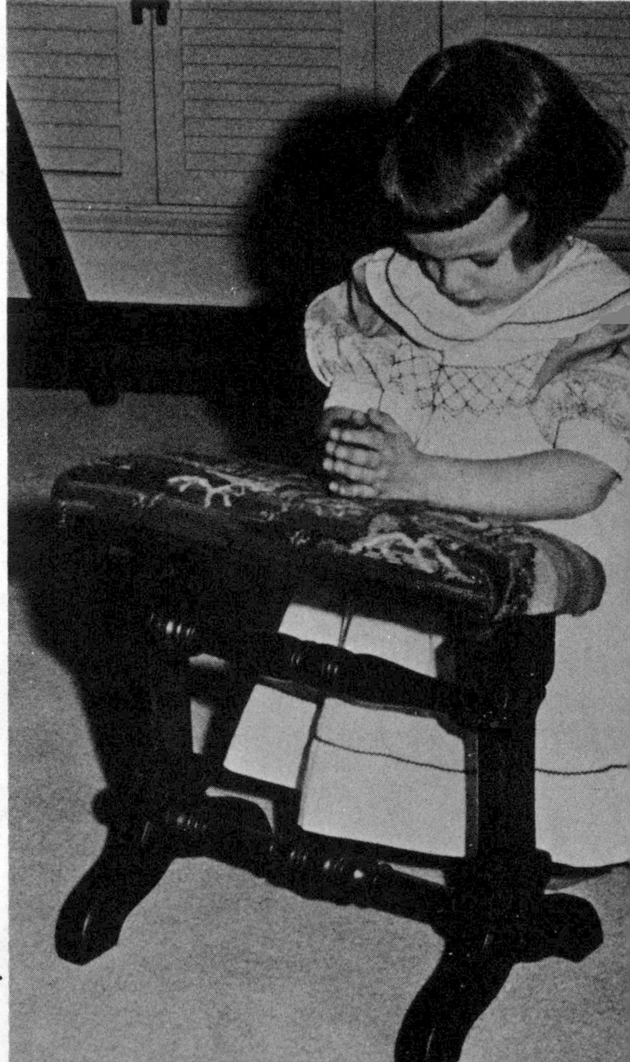

A PRAYER RAIL.

IN THE WRONG PEW.

A NEW WIFE COMES TO CHURCH.

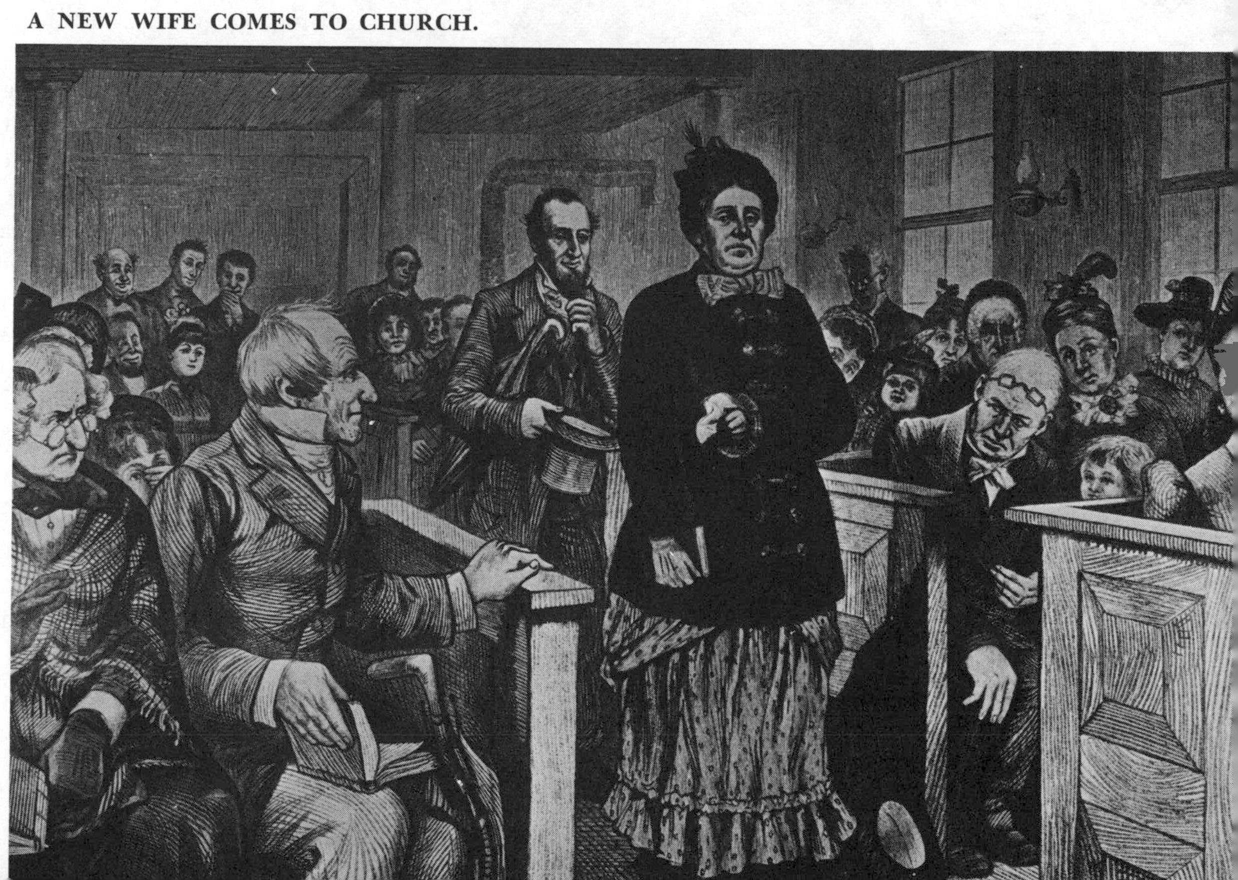

PEWS WITH DOORS.

hear the preacher, sounding boards were installed back of the pulpit in some churches to amplify his voice.

So important was religion in the early days that members of the church used to make notes of what the preacher said in his sermon and then discuss the pros and cons during the ensuing week. Thus, his utterances received thorough analysis, and the preacher whose beliefs and arguments stood up week after week became a real force and influence in the community.

The Puritans were completely absorbed in religion and fanatical about observing the Sabbath. A man wasn't even permitted to do important chores on his farm until the day was over. God's time was not to be frittered away, either, on visiting ships, window shopping, strolling down the street, or sitting under an apple tree. There was to be no cooking, bed making, sweeping, or traveling. However, it was permissible to drink perry, quince, claret, and mum, as well as rum, beer, and ale on the Sabbath.

The Puritans also were fanatically opposed to celebrating Christmas because it meant a loss of time from work and worship and a waste of energy. To them, amusement was a crime.

Schooling

The old custom of appointing only one teacher to a whole school has been generally abandoned, and the public school curriculum which once covered little more than reading, writing, arithmetic, spelling, grammar, and history has been greatly expanded.

Instead of one teacher handling all subjects and all grades in one room, we now have far-flung buildings with a corps of specialists teaching different subjects. Teachers now receive reasonably attractive salaries and live where they wish, instead of taking part of their pay in room and board and moving from one home to another in the area every week or so.

Some of the little country schools that had only one room nevertheless had two doors, one for girls and one for boys, and segregated the sexes once they got inside. The separate doors doubtless protected the girls from the sometimes unruly

THE SCHOOLHOUSE STOVE.

TEACHER'S PETS.

KEPT AFTER SCHOOL.

pushing and jostling of which boys are often guilty.

Small as they were, these little schoolhouses also served as social centers and public halls, where lyceums and debates were held. Many that still stand are serving as small and humble residences.

The teacher not only taught all grades but had to see to it that the place was kept clean and that a fire was started before school began on cold mornings. In some places the pupils either brought money to pay for the firewood (called firing money) or else their parents delivered wood in turn. Usually the boy pupils carried wood and the girls did the sweeping. There also was a pail of drinking water, used by all, to be kept full by someone.

Before pens and pencils were available, slates which could be cleaned with the wipe of a cloth and slate pencils were used for writing. Then came the copy books which taught penmanship as well as reading, followed by text books such as McGuffey's Reader.

In small communities, a teacher was under constant surveillance. She was expected to be a model of decorum, which meant abstaining from tobacco, strong alcoholic beverages, and indiscriminate masculine company.

A ONE-ROOM, TWO-DOOR SCHOOL.

DOING LESSONS ON A SLATE.

GETTING HELP FROM BROTHER.

3. Our Recreation

Work Frolics

Known also as bees and changework, work frolics were occasions when farmers got together to help a neighbor with a difficult job, to do something for the general good, or to provide an excuse to have a party.

Best known are the barn raising and house raising bees, when a young couple's neighbors turned out to help put up the frame of a new log cabin, house, or barn—heavy work that a man and his wife simply could not do all by themselves. We read also of church raising bees, school raising bees, and meeting house bees when neighbors undertook a job of benefit to them all.

A land clearing bee was another type of changework in which the group completed in a day a task that would take one man and a team of oxen many months to complete. Or the whole task might be divided into a series of bees. First there would be a logging bee when the trees would be felled, then a log rolling bee, a log piling bee, a land leveling bee, a stump pulling bee, a stone hauling bee, a wood sawing bee, a rail splitting bee, and a firewood cutting bee. While one man alone could cut up his firewood, a bee sometimes was held anyhow, just as an excuse for good fellowship.

Bees were not all work, because every now and then the group would stop for a drink of hard cider and, at the end of the day, more cider, beer, rum, and other refreshments would be served. The wives of the changeworkers would come along and spend the time at such work as quilting or carpet weaving, while the men engaged in the work frolic.

Women also held bees of their own, often just as an excuse to get together socially. They held bees for apple paring, jelly and mincemeat making, quilting, and sewing. They sewed for themselves, for the poor, or sometimes for the parson's family.

One writer observed that bees provided companionship, which was all too rare in those days, plus relaxation and

A STONE PULLING BEE.

A CORN HUSKING BEE.

A FENCING BEE.

A LOG CABIN BUILDING BEE.

the spirit of festival. The only reward for all the work done consisted of thanks from the beneficiary, plus plenty of cider, rum, and food.

Farmers also held butchering bees in cold weather and breaking-out-the-road bees in winter time when heavy snows descended and several teams of oxen were required to pull a plow through high drifts.

One of the most popular kinds of bees was the corn husking bee when the young farm folk got together in a barn or around a fire on a winter evening and husked the corn that had been harvested earlier. It was traditional on these occasions to celebrate the finding of a red ear of corn in one or both of two ways: either the finder of the red ear got to kiss the girl of his choice or else the whole group stopped for a round of cider or some other beverage. Young men who found red ears too often were suspected of planting them as a means of enjoying extra kisses.

After they had finished their work, the huskers were rewarded with refreshments such as baked beans, brown bread, pickles, apple pie, cake, coffee, and of course the usual stimulants.

In the spring and fall, farm wives would conduct a series of house cleaning bees, in order to lessen the drudgery of the job, and when nothing else needed doing they would engage in a clean-the-meeting-house bee. A good excuse for a work frolic always could be found if the lonely people really wanted to get together for work and play.

The same spirit of helpfulness also was present in the custom of sending a taster of food, called a "cold party," to neighbors after a wedding reception or other large celebration.

Entertainment

With few of the modern forms of entertainment available, everyday life could be pretty dull in the old days, so any unusual development that broke the monotony was a welcome occurrence. Thus, the hanging of a criminal, considered a gruesome spectacle today and performed in privacy, served as exciting entertainment for the whole community, as did any other form of visual punishment.

A drunk—commonly thought of as a pitiful sight—a beggar, a cripple, a man or woman in stocks—anything of the sort drew a good crowd, for want of competition.

A medicine show, a torchlight procession, a spirit meeting, a recital by the village band in the bandstand in the village square, a lyceum, a debate or Chautauqua, a showboat on the river, a hurdy gurdy or organ grinder, or a group of traveling musicians, acrobats, or actors were prime types of entertainment and drew enthusiastic crowds, as did balloon ascensions and riverboat excursions.

If there was no public event scheduled, groups would meet for singing, reading, or sewing circles, or go on a hay ride, straw ride, or sleigh ride.

In warm weather twelve to fifteen young people would take a ride in a hay wagon out into the country for dancing, donuts, and coffee under the stars. In winter they would use a sled, kept warm by straw and buffalo robes. A certain amount of courting was done on these occasions.

When nothing better loomed up, crowds of men would provoke dog fights and bet on the outcome, incite fist fights between two individuals, or stage a gan-

A STREET BAND.

THE WANDERING TRUMPET PLAYER.

STROLLING PLAYERS.

der pull. Sometimes an informal horse race could be staged on Main Street when traffic was light.

If there was absolutely nothing better to do, one could always go down to the poolhall and watch the young blades shoot a game, stop to watch the checker or domino players in the village store, saunter over to the tavern to watch the stagecoach roll in or, later on, go down to the depot to watch the fast freight go through or the local bringing passengers from the city. One could visit the corner saloon or an illegal blind pig or blind tiger for a glass of beer or a snifter. Later, during Prohibition, such a place was called a speakeasy and temporarily assumed a mantle of semi-respectability.

The boys could go for a swim at the old swimming hole, play ball on a vacant lot, hitch rides on delivery wagons or sleds, get up at dawn to meet the circus as it came to town, and then carry water to the elephants in order to earn a free admission to the great performance under the big top. It also was perfectly legal then to shoot fireworks, including cannon crackers, on the Fourth of July or any other day.

Older couples would go for a spin on their bicycles, and those of courting age went for a cozy buggy or sleigh ride out into the country.

The girls would go to slumber parties at each other's homes, couples young and old attended street dances on warm evenings or, if they resided in the larger cities, went on slumming parties to see how the poor people lived.

Frolics, cavortings, play parties, and fun makings were names for gay gatherings at which various games were played and dances such as the square dance were featured with the aid of musical instru-

ITINERANT ACROBATS.

THE HURDY-GURDY.

THE ORGAN AND THE MONKEY.

A SLUMMING PARTY.

THE OLD BANDSTAND IN THE PARK.

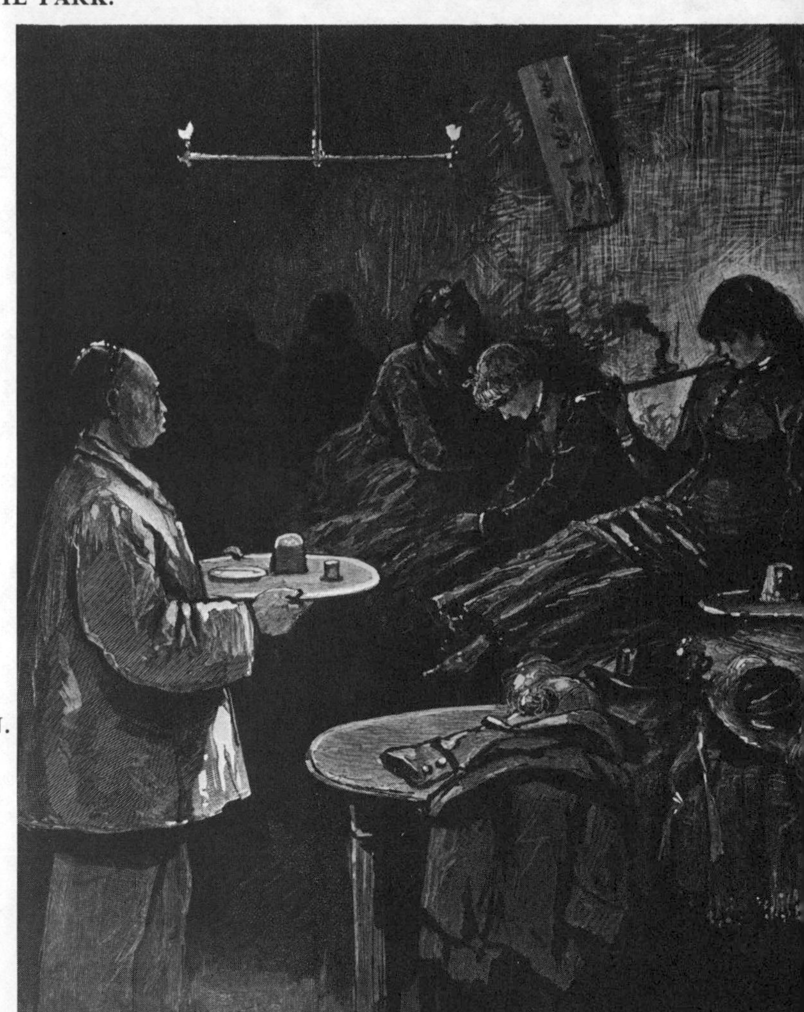

VISITING AN OPIUM DEN.

A GANDER PULL.

A SINGING CIRCLE.

A BASKET PICNIC AT THE BEACH.

A READING CIRCLE.

ments or by singing alone. In rural areas, the frolics often lasted until it was time to go home and give the cows their morning milking.

As a last resort, one could go for a brisk walk down by the river, sit on the front porch or in the living room and rock in a rocking chair, or else sit on the front steps or on a bench down by the town hall and whittle with a jackknife.

Sunday, in some parts of the country, was regarded as a "day of rest from working," which meant that recreational activities were not frowned on. The men would spend their day of rest at hunting, breaking horses, fishing, shooting at targets, jumping, wrestling, playing leap frog, foot racing, horse racing, or playing kick the hat, which involved using the hat of some member of the crowd as a football. When a rock had surreptitiously been placed under the hat, an innocent participant often wound up with a bruised or broken toe.

In the realm of musical entertainment, we are inclined to listen today rather than participate. Although we still hear an occasional piano or organ in a private home, we have to look a long way to find an old-time pump organ, upright player piano, harpsichord, melodeon, or gramophone with its big horn.

Group singing around the piano is an unusual sight these days, and all too seldom do we hear a mandolin, guitar, or banjo in the home, now that we have so much professional music free for the asking on the air waves.

The Puritans, who opposed any form of gaiety, took their meager pleasures from visiting, shooting at targets, lectures, music, eating, generous drinking, book learning, and watching punishments. Other less rigid New Englanders played at draughts, quoits, chess, skating, and sledge driving.

A RIDE ON THE BOARDWALK.

TOSSING THE DIABLO.

Games and Pastimes

There has been a great change in the kinds of games played by people of all ages. In early colonial days, of course, there was little or no time for self-entertainment. All available time was needed to keep the family supplied with bare necessities. Then, as the pressure lessened, games of many kinds gradually came into favor. The earlier card games played in the parlor were put, loo, piquet, euchre, whist, and five hundred. A dice game called paw-paw was played by men who liked to gamble, in addition to poker and other games which remain popular today.

At picnics and outings, the traditional events came to be the barrel or hogshead race, the sack race, the potato race, the egg race, catching a greased pig, and climbing a greased pole, which gave the young men a chance to show off before their lady friends.

Well-liked parlor games for people of all ages and still played by children were Lotto (a variation of Bingo), Parchesi, and such old-time favorites as. Charades, Hide the Thimble, Hunt the Whistle, Thread the Needle, Picking Cherries, Hornpipes, Trictrac, Hot Cockles, Puss in the Corner, Spin the Trencher, Up Jenkins, Simon Says Thumbs Up, Coffee Pot, Hunt the Slipper, (also known as Shuffling the Brogue), Going to Jerusalem, Honey Pots, Chuck Farthing, Philanders, Chasing the Squirrel, and Trock (variation of Billiards).

Outdoor games included I Spy, Red River, Prisoner's Base, Duck-on-a-Rock, Dog Stick, Throw the Stick, Cane Spreeing, Touchwood, Hide in the Haystack, Scotch Hoppers, Pickardel, Hoop and Hide, Tip-Cat, and Bally Cally. Pig Pile and Pom-Pom-Pullaway were rougher games played by boys and tomboys. At outings, there were beauty contests and contests for fiddlers, jumpers, wrestlers, runners, and so on.

Making popcorn and pulling taffy were popular evening pastimes, and on rainy days the young people would play in the attic or the haymow.

At weddings in the country, there was a game called Running for the Bottle, which was nothing other than a horse race staged during the reception after the wedding with a bottle of wine as a prize.

Boys spun tops and "tossed the diablo" on a cord, as did their sisters. They also played "crack the egg" at Easter. In the latter game, two boys pressed eggs together, the winner being the one whose egg didn't crack.

SPINNING A TOP.

CRACKING EGGS.

PLAYING IN THE HAY.

A FAMILY AT THE FIRESIDE.

Dancing

Social or ballroom dancing has undergone a continuing evolution through the years, with the result that today's more popular dances bear little resemblance to the folk dances that came here with our immigrants from Europe in the early days.

Occasional revivals bring back the square dances, barn dances, and Sir Roger de Coverly or Virginia Reel of some years back, and the graceful waltz and sedate one-step remain popular, but more recent favorites such as the Black Bottom, Bunny Hug, Big Apple, and Susie Q are seldom seen.

Among the popular square dances were the Money Musk, Irish Washerwoman, Fischer's Hornpipe, and Old Zip Coon.

Dancing also has tended to become more informal and, among some individuals, more intimate, in contrast to earlier times when the sedate cotillion and the cotillion leader were in vogue. Then each lady had a dance program or card on which were entered the name of each young gentleman with whom she promised to dance, bearing in mind the injunction, not always observed, which said she should never promise more than one dance to the same person.

The cotillion involved as many as two hundred and fifty figures, including the waltz, galop (known also as the one-slide racket), polka, polka Redowa, polka Mazurka, schottische, knickerbocker, five step (a mazurka with a leap and a hop), quadrille, lancers, varsovianna, two-slide racket, three-slide racket, esmeralda, society, Bohemian (a heel and toe polka), hop waltz, Boston dip, and polonaise.

One reason for the popularity of the stately minuet was the need for preserving the lavish hairdos worn by the ladies whose locks often were piled in great pyramids of paste with turbans or feathers.

One authority on the dance stated that a ball always should start with a waltz, followed by a quadrille, galop, lancers, polka, quadrille, waltz, and so on.

Other old-time dances were the jigs, including the rigadoons, Devonshire jig, and the raspies; the Spanish Fandango, and others bearing such intriguing names as the Innocent Maid, Priest's House, Clinton's Retreat, Blue Bonnet, Arcadian Nuptials, and Orange Tree.

Dancers of both sexes were counseled never to be without gloves in the ballroom.

DANCING BY CANDLELIGHT.

DANCING IN THE OLD FARMHOUSE.

AN IRISH JIG.

FORMAL DANCING.

DANCING AT A STATE FUNCTION.

Pranks

Until well after the turn of this century, many acts by youngsters that today are branded as vandalism and juvenile delinquency were regarded as mere mischief, childish pranks, or good wholesome fun, and many of the deeds that were viewed with tolerance if not amusement in those days would today lead the perpetrators to juvenile court, boy's training school, or at least probation.

Halloween was the time when these pranks were most likely to be performed. It was taken for granted then that front gates would be removed and perhaps hung on the church steeple, privies would be overturned, and weak fences would be pulled over.

Fun-loving boys would tie a string to two cans and place one on each side of the sidewalk so that pedestrians would trip in the dark and drag them along with their feet, and buckets of water would be suspended above doorways to spill when the doors opened.

Boys would place pins in doorbells so they would ring continuously, or ring a doorbell and then run before the owner could open the door and catch them. They would throw corn against windowpanes to frighten the occupants of a house and write on the windows with soap. Sometimes the corn throwing was done on a special night, known as corn night, one or two days ahead of Halloween as a sort of warm-up. The same was true of tick-tack night when spools with notches in the ends would be placed on a pencil or small stick and revolved against first-floor windows with the aid of a string wound around them.

People hardly paid any attention at all to shooting at weathervanes and signboards and sawing lightpoles halfway through so they would tumble in a strong wind.

In addition to the usual special atten-

RAIDING THE COOKIE JAR.

REMOVING A CAN FROM A DOG'S TAIL.

"OPEN YOUR MOUTH AND SHUT YOUR EYES AND I'LL GIVE YOU SOMETHING TO MAKE YOU WISE."

tions at Halloween, any citizen who incurred the ill will of a group of youngsters by spoiling their fun or being too cranky could expect such retribution as having his front door painted with syrup to attract bugs and flies, having stray cats put inside his back door, or being pelted with snowballs.

Other "pranks" which have been pretty well stamped out included tying a tin can to a dog's tail to frighten him when he ran; painting the rear end of a dog with turpentine, causing him to rush around in a frenzy; dipping a girl's long tresses into an inkwell on the school desk back of her, and putting tacks on the chair seat of a teacher or schoolmate.

Milder pranks consisted of harassing sister and her boy friend by scaring them with pumpkin faces, firecrackers, animal noises, and the like. Even grandpa wasn't immune from a little scaring when fireworks were around.

In larger communities, at least, it no longer is the practice to kidnap a bride after the wedding, so as to worry the bridegroom, and we no longer hear much about the shivaree. Known also as a charivari or callithump, the shivaree was a prolonged serenade of loud noises and cat calls beneath the bedroom windows of a newly married couple. Horns, drums, kettles, whistles, and other noise makers were employed to keep the young couple awake and force them to appear at the window and perhaps admit the crowd for refreshments. This "prank" was great fun fcr all but the bride and groom.

SALTING THE SLIDE.

SCARING A SUITOR.

STEALING A WATERMELON.

SCARING GRANDPA.

INTERRUPTING A PROPOSAL.

A SHIVAREE.

4. Our Homes

House and Yard

The kitchen is the only room in the American home that has remained unchanged in name and function through the years, although in the early days it also served other functions.

In humble homes it once served as the bedroom, and after bedrooms were added the kitchen continued as the living room, the place where the family spent its leisure time and did its reading, writing, mending, carding, knitting, spinning, weaving, and sewing.

The living room, which did not appear until houses began to grow in size, once was better known as the sitting room. Its companion—the parlor—which was located just inside the front door, was variously called the front room, company room, fore room, and keeping room. The sitting room was the one in which the family relaxed, while the parlor, which had the best haircloth furniture and furnishings, was kept in apple pie order at all times in case of unexpected company and for scheduled entertaining.

Some large homes also had a third first-floor room called a library, if it had a lot of books and a big desk, or a den if its main feature was a large easy chair used only by Dad, the one in which he took his post-dinner and Sunday afternoon naps. That chair was either a Morris chair with an adjustable back or else a well padded leather chair.

Upstairs, besides the bedrooms, there often were a sewing room and a guest room or spare room. These in reality were extra bedrooms, the kind that became available for other purposes when the kids grew up and moved to homes of their own.

These rooms had no closets; instead, they had massive free-standing cabinets called wardrobes, which were equipped with single or double doors, with or without mirrors.

Space for bathrooms, a development of the late 1800's in most homes, was found by taking over smaller bedrooms and dividing them into bathrooms and closets.

Above the bedrooms was that super-handy storage space known as the garret

UP IN THE ATTIC.

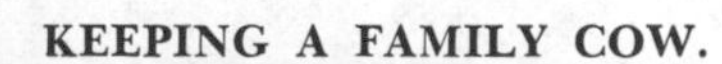

KEEPING A FAMILY COW.

or third floor or attic. In many homes, it became a treasure chest as Mother stowed there all the old possessions that were deemed too good to throw away but too old or useless to retain precious space down below.

Every home of any consequence had several stairways. There was the main front stairway leading up from the front hall to the second floor hall, and the narrower back stairs which led from the kitchen up to the second floor hallway back near the maid's room. This was the avenue of escape for Mother if caught downstairs in a wrapper when the Preacher came to call. She would dash up the back stairs to her bedroom, unseen by anyone in the front of the house, and then make a stately appearance down the front stairs when she had donned her company attire.

Before the disappearing stairway came along, there was an attic stairway, like the back stairs narrower and steeper than the front stairs, and also the cellar stairs which led to the basement. The latter also tended to be steep and narrow and poorly lighted as well. That is where lazy people put scrub pails, brooms, mops, and other articles to serve as booby traps instead of carrying them down below. There also were outside steps leading to the porches and down into the basement area or into the root cellar.

In the basement were the large coal furnace, the unsightly coal bin, the ash tubs, and various outmoded bits of equipment too cumbersome to be put in the attic. The cellar was a place to avoid in the days when grimy coal was the principal household fuel.

Next to the kitchen was the pantry, now superseded by continuous counters and kitchen cabinets, in which Mother kept her dishes, glasses, and a stock of non-perishable foods and did some of her

A "MODERN" BATHROOM.

A RAIN BARREL.

A SUN DIAL.

food preparation. If the home was a really grand one, it also had a butler's pantry, in which the butler or cook or dining-room maid could make salads, lay out the tableware, and stack soiled dishes as they were removed from the table. The butler's pantry saved steps for whoever waited on the table, reduced congestion in the kitchen, and usually had a small sink and running water for preliminary dish washing and for drink mixing.

Inside doors often had transoms, small windows above the doors which permitted ventilation and the entrance of light into a room when the door was closed. Electric lights and fans and air conditioning have made transoms unnecessary.

Outside the house proper, one occasionally found a summer kitchen where food could be cooked in hot weather without heating up the house, a conservatory or sun room, sometimes part of the house, where flowers were grown, and a wood shed or closet which often was on the back porch and held sticks of wood to be used in interior fireplaces and, earlier, in the kitchen fireplace and stove.

Then, there were the porches: the large front porch—called a piazza or veranda—was frequently screened in, with its wooden swing hung by chains from the ceiling. The front porch frequently extended clear across the front of the house and turned a corner along one side or else ended in a porte-cochere, a sheltered place where carriages and, later, automobiles could discharge their passengers. Other smaller porches on the back and side of the house were known as stoops, except for the roomier back porch which was roofed over.

In those days, residential areas in towns and cities almost always had sidewalks for pedestrians and back alleys for the use of service vehicles like garbage wagons, delivery wagons, and the ashman.

In horse and buggy days a driveway typically led from the street through a pair of stately gate posts, under the porte-cochere, and on back to the stable or carriage house located on an alley at the back of the lot.

If there was no alley, the carriage house was located alongside the house on the street but was separated by a garden and a stone walk. Nowadays, of course, the patio in the rear of the house and the garage have replaced the front porch and the stable, even in many older homes that have been remodeled to meet today's living preferences.

Especially in rural areas, each home had a root cellar, a below-ground storage area often under the house, entered from the outside by double or single hinged doors, in which were stored apples, potatoes, turnips, parsnips, carrots, preserves, and the various barrels and boxes in which nonperishable foods were brought from the store.

At a corner of the house under a downspout was a rain barrel that caught the rain which came off the roof and kept it for washing purposes. Larger homes had a cistern, a large, brick-lined hole into which the rain-water flowed, giving the family a supply of extra-soft water. A sundial, bird bath, and a pump or well completed the outdoor equipment, except for the front fence and the

A SUMMER KITCHEN.

THE BACK ALLEY.

wooden gate on which the kids used to swing for want of anything better to do and where sister used to say a lingering goodbye to her boy friend after he had carried her books home from school.

If there was no sun dial, there often was a noon mark on a window sill or threshold to give some idea of the time of day in the absence of a clock or pocket watch.

The yard, in towns and cities as well as on farms, often included a chicken yard or coop and a small cow barn, for the custom of keeping a cow for milk and chickens for eggs was quite general. Most yards also had a few apple, cherry, and peach trees and at least a small vegetable garden and corn patch, plus some raspberry bushes and perhaps a patch of strawberries. Families in the older days were much more self-sufficient than they are today.

Home Equipment

Grandfather's home had a great many pieces of equipment, furnishings, and decorations that have disappeared with the years. It had, for example, framed mottoes hanging on the walls that said, "God Bless Our Home," "In God, We Trust," "Peace Be With You," "Home, Sweet Home," and "Love One Another." One motto read, "In prosperity, friends will be plenty, In adversity, not one in twenty."

The parlor or living room would have a highbacked, haircloth sofa, pillows filled with pine needles, some rag carpets, several rocking chairs, a cuspidor, a quilting frame, a prayer stool, a spinning wheel, a large family Bible, several kerosene lamps, some candlesticks, and perhaps a pump organ or harpsichord.

In the kitchen, in addition to the wooden icebox, the dry sink, the chair table, and the iron range, you usually could find a nutmeg grater, metal canisters holding tea and coffee, a coffee grinder, a teapot with a knitted cozy surrounding it, a cheese press, a dough-raising box, a woodbox, and a coal scuttle. In the real early days, there would be several tankards, made of wood or pewter for drinking beer, ale, and other beverages, and sometimes extensively decorated; a rummer for quaffing rum; a pewter charger or platter, a wooden trencher on which to carve and serve the meat, and a wooden breadboard for slicing bread at the dining table. Often food and herbs were hung up to dry on long rails.

The fully equipped kitchen also had a slate with crayon and eraser so that menus could be written for the cook on one side and items needed from the store on the other.

AN UMBRELLA STAND.

A BOOTSCRAPER.

LONELY ROCKING CHAIRS.

A PUMP ORGAN.

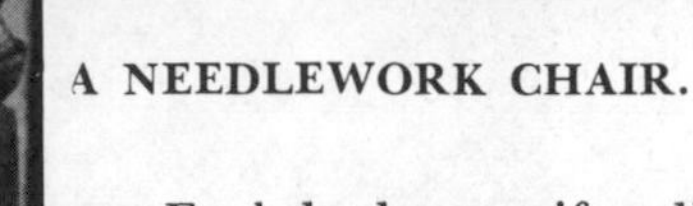

A NEEDLEWORK CHAIR.

Each bedroom, if well equipped, had a brass bedstead, a spool bed, or maybe a canopy bed; several homemade comfortables or comforters and quilts; a mattress filled with chicken or goose feathers or a bedtick filled with corn leaves and stalks or other reasonably soft material; a chamber pot under the bed; a wash stand with slop jar, pitcher, and bowl; a clothes tree, and a small rag rug. The bed springs consisted of a network of corded ropes, which were kept tight with the aid of a special tool.

In bedrooms and elsewhere, one found wall pockets or bags in which one

Until our modern kitchen conveniences and our great array of canned and frozen foods came along, the home kitchen was a veritable factory—the scene of much cutting, slicing, mixing, blending, kneading, grinding, and so on—as the housewife performed many of the functions assumed by the food manufacturer today. And she had a great array of implements with which to carry out her culinary tasks. Getting meals was real work in those days, since every recipe had to be made up from ingredients in their natural state.

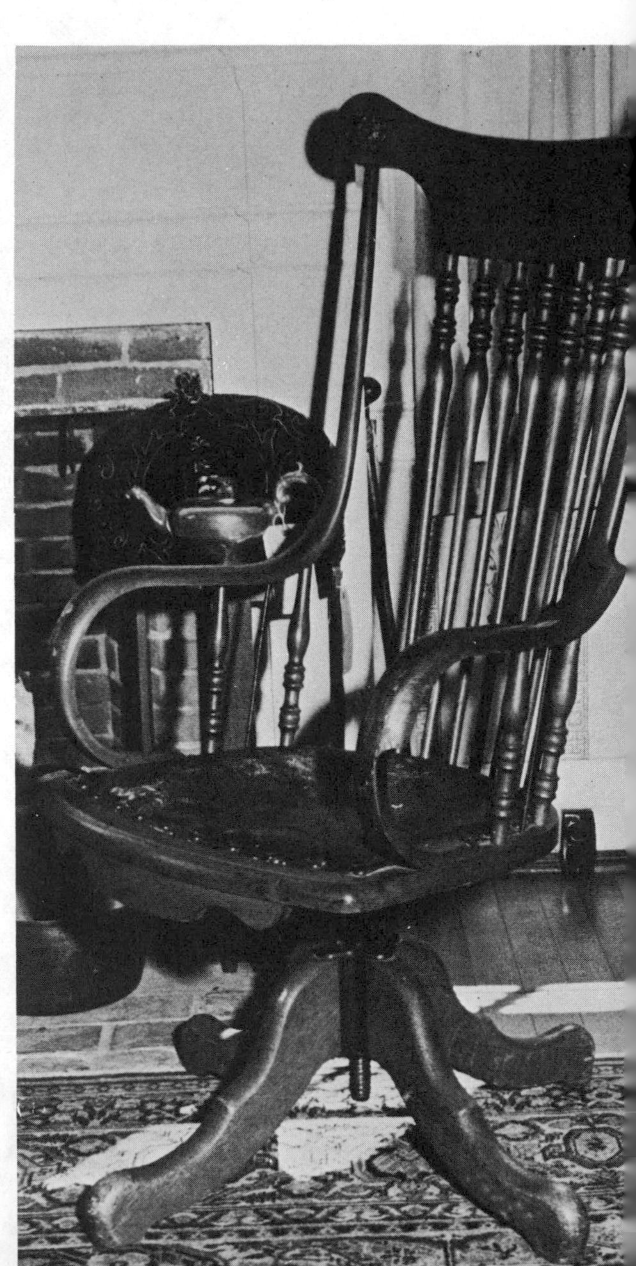

GRANDPA'S OLD DESK CHAIR.

A ROLLTOP DESK.

A HATRACK.

put odds and ends and minor belongings so the room would look neater.

In the back hall, hanging on hooks, were some lanterns, a carpet beater, and market basket. Hanging on a hatrack near the front door were hats, bonnets, capes, and other garments for outside wear. Underneath was an umbrella rack holding umbrellas, parasols, and canes.

DRYING FOOD.

DRYING HERBS.

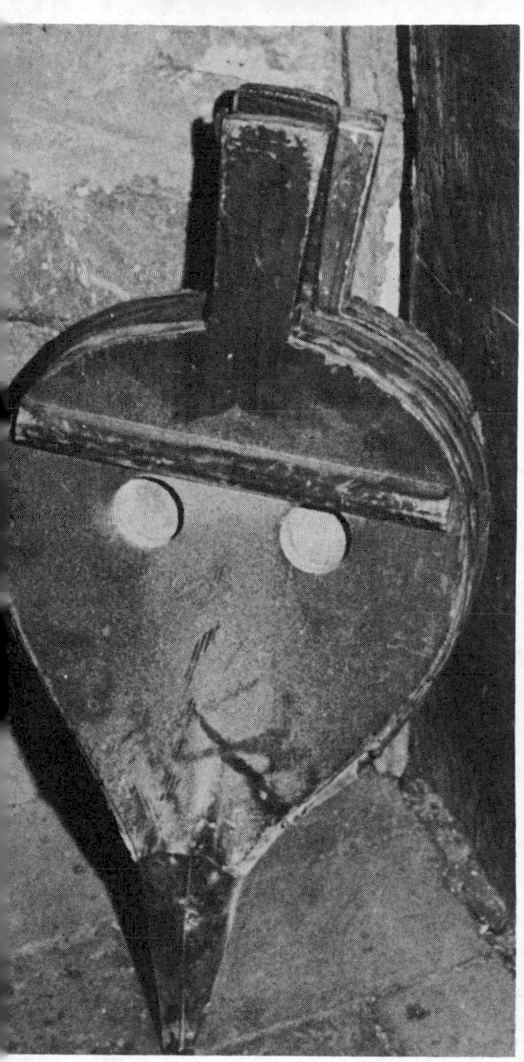

A BELLOWS.

A TANKARD.

Home Lighting

Flipping a switch to light a room, like turning a faucet to get water, is a relatively recent innovation—a far cry from the days when pine knots, whale oil, candles, kerosene, and illuminating gas were used.

Pine knots, obtained from pitch pine trees, were a very early means of lighting, along with dried reeds soaked in fat, both of which gave a flickering light and smoked too much. Bayberry or candleberry oil and whale oil were used in a shallow dish with a string hanging down the side to serve as a wick. However, the candle, or tallow dip, made of spermaceti, tallow, wax, or paraffin, was the first generally used source of interior illumination.

The candles usually were made in the home by the housewife, who carefully saved every scrap of household grease for the purpose, accumulated tallow from slaughtered farm animals, and knitted her own wicks out of cotton thread. She used special moulds which enabled her to make as many as a dozen candles at one time, or else dipped wicks repeatedly in bowls of melted tallow.

The use of candles required candlesticks to hold the one candle used to illuminate small rooms and to light the way up to bed at night; sconces or candle arms holding several candles which were hung on the wall; candle beams or chandeliers, candle stands, and candle holders or boxes in which extra candles and candle ends were kept. Also needed were snuffers, known also as snuffing irons and snits, to put out the candles and wick trimmers which cut off the burned ends of the wicks.

Kerosene lamps, which came along

A CANDLESTAND.

A CANDLE REFLECTOR.

after the discovery of petroleum in this country, took the form of small single lamps, used like a candle to light the way around the house after dark, as well as larger lamps with shades to throw light down onto a table and chandeliers having a half dozen or more individual kerosene lamps to light a whole room.

When kerosene lamps were used, someone had to service them every day, which meant adding kerosene, trimming wicks, and cleaning the glass chimneys with rags or newspapers.

When cooking was done by wood in fireplaces and stoves and home lighting was provided by candles and kerosene, each family tried to keep some coals burning in order to permit the lighting of fires, lamps, and candles. If the fire went out, someone had to run to a neighbor and borrow some coals in a shovel or bed warmer or else laboriously try to get a spark with a flint and steel firemaker.

Most homes had a metal box in which they kept scraps of old linen called tinder, to catch these sparks, together with the flint and steel, with the top of the tinder box often serving as a candlestick. When burning coals were available, small twisted pieces of paper called

A CANDLESTICK.

A CANDLE SNUFFER.

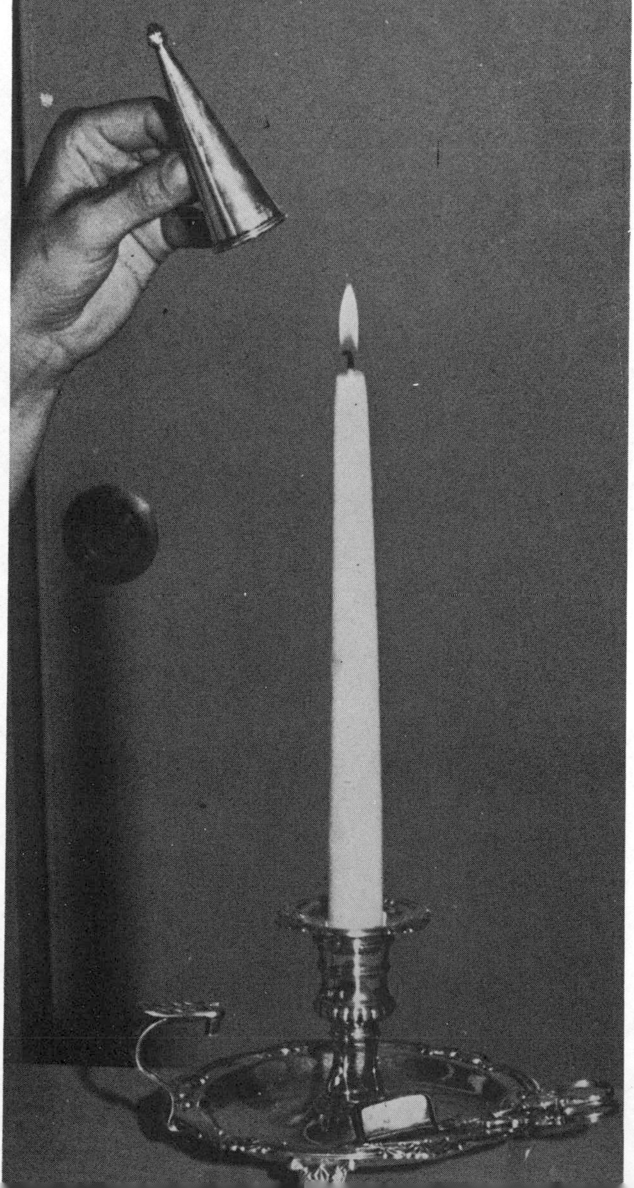

A WICK TRIMMER.

spills were used to transfer the flame from stove to fireplace, candle, or lamp.

By the time illuminating gas came along to replace everything that had been used earlier for general home lighting, matches had been introduced, and you lit the burners by hand, using a waxed wick called a taper, held in a long wood and metal handle, to reach burners placed high on the wall or hanging from the ceiling. The holder also was equipped to turn off the gas when the light no longer was needed.

Since the gas was toxic to human beings, care had to be exercised to see that a gas light wasn't accidentally blown out, thus releasing unburnt gas in a room. It was this danger that led to the early replacement of gas light by electricity.

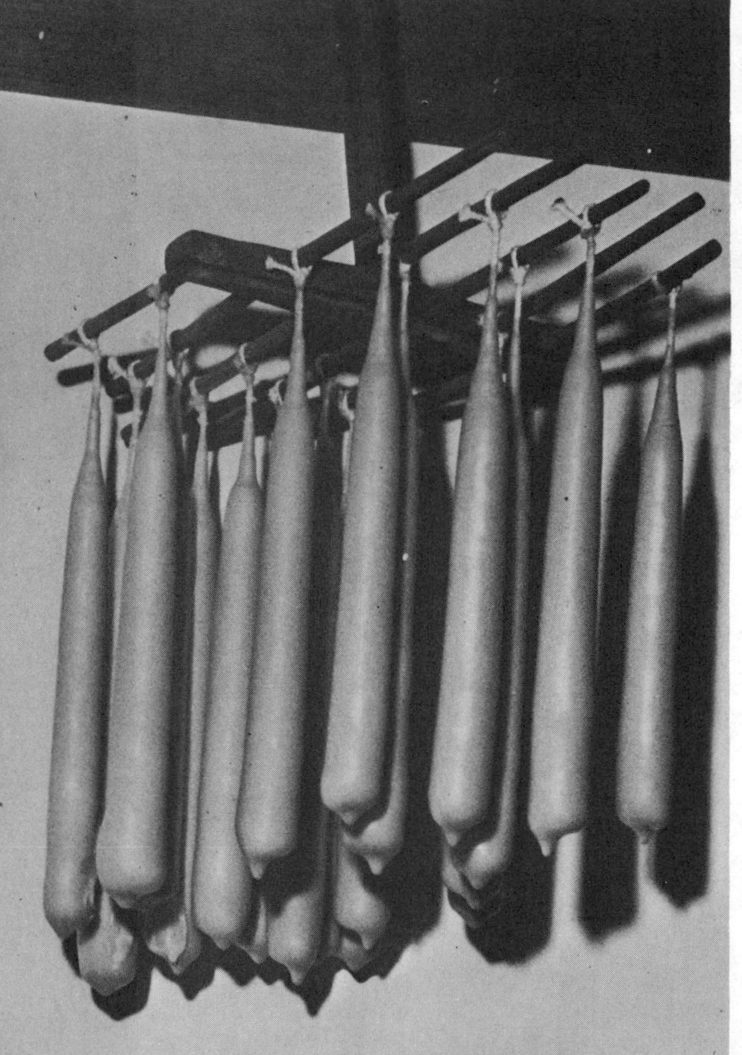

DIPPED CANDLES.

OUTSIDE CANDLE LIGHT.

A KEROSENE LAMP.

A LIVING ROOM STOVE.

Home Heating

From the crude open fireplaces of log cabin days to the automatic gas and oil furnaces of today, home heating has undergone a great change.

The large wood-burning fireplace, located in the principal room of the cabin or in the kitchen if there was one, served to provide heat for warmth and cooking, plus light for interior illumination and reading. With its long crane, its pots and kettles, its oven built into the back wall, and its trivets, bellows, and other equipment, the fireplace was a vital part of the early-day home. Prominent in the list of other equipment were the trammels or pothooks, also known as hakes, clams, claws, clips, brakes, hangers, and crooks. These hung first from a log-pole, and then from a long crane. In front of the hearth was a sheltered bench, known as a warming bench, where the family enjoyed the warmth of the fireside on cold evenings.

As houses grew in size, smaller fireplaces were added to warm bedrooms and living rooms, the fuel being wood or, in some places, coal.

Eventually the big kitchen range made of iron with its ovens, its lids and lid lifters, and stovepipe replaced the open fireplace for cooking. Heating then was accomplished with the aid of small stoves, including Franklin stoves and potbellied stoves which made more efficient use of the fuel when placed in or in front of fireplaces.

Since it was not customary in those frugal days to heat rooms when they were not in use, bedrooms got mighty cold in wintertime and, when it came time to retire, long-handled warming pans were placed between the sheets to

TO KEEP FOOD WARM.

A LARGE KITCHEN FIREPLACE.

warm the beds before the occupants arrived.

Bedrooms were equally cold on frosty winter mornings and, after reluctantly leaving a warm bed, everyone rushed to the kitchen fireplace or stove in the hope that there would be enough smoldering coals from the night before to start up a blaze when kindling was added.

As houses grew larger, a need for central heating arose, and it first was provided by means of a coal-burning furnace in the basement which sent heat up through an opening or register centrally located in the first floor. Later, hot air was piped to each room through registers in the floor or wall, as is the case today with gas and oil furnaces.

Use of a coal furnace meant there had to be a coal bin in the basement near the furnace, and there had to be coal shovels, ashcans, pokers, and other accessories. The furnace had to be stoked and banked at night, grates had to be shaken, clinkers had to be broken up, and ashes had to be removed from the furnace and carried outside in ashcans. In those days, there was a lot more to keeping a home warm than just moving the indicator on a thermostat.

THE OLD IRON STOVE.

Household Workers

One of our most prominent authorities on household management said not too many years ago that the complete minimum home service organization consisted of a cook, housemaid, and butler or waiter, adding that a laundress was desirable. The butler, this authority stated, could act as a housekeeper in full command.

Also desirable, the advisor went on, were a chambermaid, parlor maid, footman or useful man, scullery maid, coachman, gardener, nursemaid, and undercook, to which might be added a companion, a private secretary, and a social secretary. Obviously, the latter would fit only into a reasonably large establishment. It will be noted that the expanded list fails to mention a valet, lady's maid, upstairs maid, and pantrymaid, once found in most really large homes.

All of this, of course, was in the days when wages were appallingly low and household labor was in over-supply as a result of the flood of immigrants from Europe.

A PARLOR MAID.

A SERVING GIRL.

THE USEFUL MAN.

One authority pointed out that, in a small home, the butler worked more with his hands than his head. He was custodian of the wine cellar and of the key to the silver safe. Among other duties, he assisted the head of the house with his coat and handed him his hat and stick, which previously had been handed to him—the butler—by the footman. It is noted by another authority that first-class butlers and footmen do *not* wear moustaches.

The coachman performed other duties in addition to driving the family horses and caring for the vehicles. He sometimes acted as messenger, gardener, and furnace man and did odd jobs from time to time.

Before the automatic washer and dryer became commonplace, the family which did not employ a full-time or part-time laundress used to send the laundry out to a washerwoman who did the work in her home. Often it was called for and delivered in a small wooden wagon, known as an express wagon, by her husband, or more often by a son or daughter.

In Philadelphia in the early days, occupants of homes were required to sweep the street half way across every day and to wash the sidewalk daily. Where no servant was available, this was a job for the housewife.

However, household servants were not hard to obtain. If he couldn't hire a suitable person, a householder used to be able to obtain the services of an indentured servant who, instead of paying for his passage, permitted himself to be sold into service for a stated period, usually three to seven years, by the owner or master of the ship that transported him to this country from Europe.

Craftsmen also used to obtain helpers in this way, agreeing to teach a man a specified trade in return for his services over a period of years during which the craftsman agreed to support the indentured man as well as teach the trade. Upon completion of the term of indenture, the master was obligated to provide the man with clothing, land, and other perquisites to help him get started on his own.

Another source of household help consisted of young children who acted as servants in a home in return for receiving an education. And paupers, includ-

A CARELESS MAID.

CAUGHT IN THE ACT.

ing old people, used to be sold into bondage for terms of a year or more by the courts as a means of providing for their support.

Not all homes had household employees, of course, but it has been said that every middle-class family had at least a part-time domestic helper in the latter part of the nineteenth century and in the early part of the present century.

A LADY'S MAID.

BAGGAGE INSPECTION.

Baggage

In the days when most traveling was by railroad and ship, trunks of all sizes were widely used to transport personal effects. There was the small steamer trunk designed to fit under berths on steamships and the huge Saratoga trunk, which could hold almost an entire wardrobe. There was the horsehide trunk or hair trunk, made of leather with the hair of the animal left in place. While some people had trunks made of deerhide and pigskin, others used less pretentious wooden cases, fitted with hinges and locks.

However, people also carried hand luggage, including the cardboard suitcase, an inexpensive container with a handle, made of cardboard, and the carpetbag, made of a piece of old carpet or perhaps of new carpet-like material.

Other hand luggage consisted of the reticule, which was a network bag; the bandbox, a light container of wood or cardboard to hold collars, hats, caps, et cetera—a sort of hat box—and the satchel, grip, or valise, an upright bag with a collapsible top favored by men who traveled a good deal.

A LEATHER TRUNK AND HAT BOX.

A FANCY TRUNK.

A SARATOGA TRUNK.

5. Our Food and Drink

Everyday Dining

Breakfasts have not always consisted of orange juice, toast, donuts, pancakes, ham and eggs, and coffee. In New England in colonial days, the morning meal used to be meat, fish or cheese, and bread. Later the menu was expanded to include fried potatoes, Johnny cake, sausage, oatmeal or rye hash rolls, buttermilk biscuits, plain or cider applesauce, and twisted molasses donuts, with honey and maple syrup in place of sugar for the coffee.

Items served for the morning meal down South in the 1800's were gravy toast, baked sweet potato, banana toast, rice with lentil dressing, and roasted almonds. Breakfast in Philadelphia used to take up to one and a half hours so great was the variety of food served.

A Virginia breakfast was described as including wheaten rolls, apple bread, honey, hominy, and herring. Mince pie, eaten for dinner, rather than breakfast, often contained bear meat. Another delicacy was dandelion greens prepared the way turnip greens are today in the South, with ham hock and sowbelly, served in vinegar and butter.

A good Quaker dinner might consist of "ducks, hams, chickens, beef, pig, tarts, creams, custards, jellies, trifles, fools, floating island, beer, porter, punch, and wine," or "turtle, flummers, sillies, sweetmeats of twenty sorts, trifles, whipped sillabubs, fruit, raisins, almonds, pears, and parmesan cheese," plus a wide assortment of beverages.

At a Christmas dinner in Philadelphia some years later, the menu included "roast beef, veal, turkey, ducks, fowls, hams, puddings, jellies, oranges, apples, nuts, almonds, figs, raisins, and various wines and punches."

Then the menu of one Thanksgiving dinner in old New England included "dried cherries, haunch of venison, chine of roast pork, roast turkey, roast goose, pigeon patties, an abundance of good vegetables, Indian pudding, sellery, mince pie, pumpkin pie, apple tarts, suet

WAITING FOR A FAMILY DINNER.

THE YOUNGSTERS STOOD UP.

pudding, dried plumbs, preserved ginger, nuts, and oranges."

In very early days, drinking water was served at the table in a bucket with a gourd, and all courses were put on the table at once. In some families, everyone ate out of one dish. Even in Queen Victoria's time, it was customary to place a whole loaf of bread on the table with a knife so the loaf could be sliced as needed.

Young folk and women, too, often ate at a second table if there were too many important men for the first sitting. In some families, children stood at meals, behind adults or at a separate table. Dogs often roamed about the room, scavenging under the table for dropped bones and other morsels.

In other homes, family members and servants ate together, with the latter sitting at the far end of the table below the large salt boat or saltcellar which was kept in the center, sometimes in a caster which also held pepper, vinegar, mustard, and nutmeg.

Anyone having dinner before eight o'clock ran the risk of being thought stodgy, because, as one authority put it, "only quiet folk eat before eight."

To prevent boredom at the table, families were urged to select a special topic of conversation for each meal, announcing the subject in advance "so that even the youngest family member would have the opportunity to prepare himself."

Even in the early days there was concern about the feeding of children. In one old cookbook, we read that "The cow selected to provide the milk for an infant should be between the ages of four and ten and should be of mild disposition. She should be fed on good, clean grain and hay, free from must. She should be cleaned and cared for like a carriage horse and milked twice a day, preferably by the same person at the same time."

BREAKING THE WISHBONE.

Formal Dining

In formal dining, as elsewhere, customs change with the times. Today, for example, we no longer see the little menu that was recommended for the formal dinner back around 1880. It appeared either on small porcelain slates, one between each two diners, or on hand-printed cards. Listed were the principal foods to be served, but it was not deemed necessary to include such obvious items as celery, radishes, olives, bread and butter, or mints.

The hand-made menu card offered much opportunity for adding attraction to a company dinner, according to one etiquette book, if the hostess possessed the necessary artistic skill. She was advised to paint a floral decoration or tiny sketch with an appropriate quotation on each card, along with the guest's name and the date of the dinner. Such a card made a very pleasing souvenir. A proper quotation printed after each dish was described as being "much in vogue as a means of stimulating conversation between guests," and it was best if the quotations were all taken from one author.

Ladies were advised to keep their fan and gloves in their lap when sitting down at the table, and the hostess was told that a foot stool under the table for each lady would add greatly to their comfort and make it easier for them to keep the fan and gloves from slipping to the floor.

It was customary in those days to place a dinner roll on the napkin of each guest to be munched while waiting for the first course or, if preferred, the roll could be replaced by a piece of bread two and one-half inches long and one and one-half inches thick. It was considered ill-bred to wait for others to be served, so each guest was advised to start eating as soon as served.

To make sure that no guest was slighted, it was the practice for the hostess to talk first with the guest on her right and then to the one on her left. When she shifted her attention, known as "the turn of the table," other guests were supposed to follow her example. Anyone who did not do so ran the risk of causing the hostess to remind him of his error by suspending conversation and looking his way.

When food came with seeds, the diner was advised to cover his or her lips with his or her hand, drop the seeds unseen into the palm, and then deposit them on the side of the plate. Rather than place a finger bowl and napkin at each place, some hostesses provided one bowl which was passed from person to person by a servant or by the guests themselves. Those who used the bowl first naturally enjoyed the clearest water.

Before women began to smoke cigarettes, it was customary for the men to withdraw to the smoking room for a half hour after dinner. There, cigars and brandy were passed to the male guests.

Dinners used to last up to three hours which led to much over-eating, because as one observer put it, "you had to keep on eating to stay awake."

The introduction of the fork and spoon to supplement the knife in eating required, or at least led to, new emphasis on table etiquette and a new set of table manners, some of them contradictory. For example, some people held to the idea that one should never leave a spoon in a cup or glass because of the likelihood that an arm and elbow would hit the spoon and knock over the container.

But some authorities advised that the right way to turn down a second cup of tea or coffee was to leave the spoon in the cup as a signal that no more was wanted. Others recommended turning the cup upside down. To reject a second helping of food, one approved method was to cross one's knife and fork on the plate.

It was perfectly proper to offer to share a large pear with a lady at the table, but a man did not pare an apple or pear for a lady unless requested to do so and then he used his fork to hold the fruit.

A TOOTHPICK DISPENSER.

One approved way to facilitate the eating of peas with a knife, in the absence of a fork, was to put honey on the knife. And if one felt impelled to pick his teeth at the table, he was told to hold his napkin before his mouth with his free hand. Another authority said a person never should use his knife or fork for picking his teeth. Some thoughtful hostesses provided special toothpick holders on the table.

It is interesting to note that before the introduction of the fork hostesses were obliged to keep a much larger stock of napkins than is required today, because the hands came in contact with food much more often.

"Never throw bones under the dinner table," one authority advised, adding that when sending a plate for a second helping, one should retain the knife and fork and place them on a piece of bread until the plate was returned.

Water Supply

Getting a good, wholesome drink of water, a pot of water for tea or coffee, or a few gallons of water for laundering or bathing hasn't always been so easy.

Out in the country, you got your water by dipping it from a nearby spring, using a well sweep, raising a pailful with a crank, or pumping it by hand from a well, although windmills later eased the labor on many farms. For most rural people, running water in the home did not come until gasoline and electric driven pumps were installed.

In towns, there often was a town pump where everyone got his water, but in congested city areas, where water tended to be of questionable purity,

THE VILLAGE PUMP.

A WOODEN PUMP.

GOING TO FETCH A PAIL OF WATER.

even the poorer people bought drinking water from vendors who offered spring water from special horse-drawn carts. Water for tea or coffee could be purchased in small quantities, and water for general drinking purposes was sold from casks by the quart and gallon.

Public water had to be boiled for drinking in many places until recently and, of course, boiling still is deemed advisable in areas that have been flooded.

Milk, too, was sold by the pail from house to house, having been hauled to town by farmers in open buckets.

SELLING DRINKING WATER.

A CIDERPRESS.

Beverages

The merits of water as a beverage were suspect in the early days, so the settlers relied to a great extent on cider, beer, ale, rum, and wine to satisfy their thirsts at mealtime and in between.

Some who write of early times assert that our forefathers drank entirely too much of these alcoholic beverages and that they—at least the men—were semi-intoxicated, if not drunk, a good deal of the time. Children, as well as adults, drank freely of hard cider, according to reports. Even preachers were said to have barrels of cider stored in their homes, though perhaps some form of preservative was added to prevent it from turning hard.

The liquor bills for celebrations such as those held when a new church was completed often ran into rather high figures.

Almost every town had a cider press where farmers took their apples to be pressed each fall, and larger farms had their own private presses. Cider was so common that it was served gratis to tramps as well as more welcome visitors, just as a housewife offers a cup of coffee today to persons calling at her home.

Drunken people were a problem almost everywhere. Wheelbarrows were used to transport them to jail or to the stocks where they were confined until they sobered up. The expression, "climbing on the water wagon," which meant giving up alcohol, came into being later on when water wagons were seen on city streets selling drinking and cooking water.

Places specializing in selling rum and wine for off-premises consumption were known as rum shops or tippling shops, although in earlier days alcoholic beverages for home use were sold in grocery stores.

All of the popular beverages were, of course, consumed unmixed and undiluted, but there also were a number of mixed drinks, most of which have gradually disappeared. One was grog, a plain mixture of rum and water, best known for its popularity in the British Navy. Mumbo was rum and water with sugar added. Other rum drinks were the stone-

A TOPER.

AN UNFORTUNATE INEBRIATE.

wall (rum and hard cider), the calibogus (cold rum and beer), and the switchell (rum, water, molasses, and vinegar).

Rum fustian consisted of rum, beer, sherry, gin, eggs, and nutmeg and was drunk from large containers made of silver, pewter, and sometimes wood. There was a great variety of rum punches, rum having been the most widely used beverage of high alcoholic content before corn whisky became popular.

Both men and women who were fastidious about their drinks carried nutmegs in small silver containers equipped with built-in graters to flavor their wines and punches.

Flip, another favorite, was concocted of either beer or cider, plus rum, molasses, and syrup, heated by the insertion of a red-hot iron tool with a long handle and a ball on the end known as a loggerhead, and also called a flip-iron and flip-dog. The expression, "They were at loggerheads," was one way of saying that two individuals were in disagreement and were using loggerheads as weapons.

Negus, best known in New Orleans, contained wine, hot water, sugar, nutmeg, and lemon juice.

A scotcher contained applejack, boiled water, and mustard. Treacle, used as an antidote for snake bite or poison, was a mixture of herbs, drugs, wine, and honey or molasses. The list of old-time drinks also includes the rumbullion, kill-devil, spruce, shrub, and sangaree.

The various beverages were quaffed from mugs, steins, flagons, tankards, caudle cups, posset cups, and dram cups.

A mild beverage known as sack posset, served to brides and grooms at wedding parties and at christenings, consisted of sack or sherry, sugar, nutmeg, milk, and egg. Metheglin, known also as mead, was made of fermented honey and water, while arak was distilled from rice and molasses.

Before the day of canned and bottled beer, it was customary to buy the beverage by the pail or pitcher, and sending a child or servant out to the corner saloon for a fresh supply was known as "rushing the growler." Later, in the era of Prohibition and the speakeasy, when there was no such thing as today's bar-and-grill, drinkers carried pocket flasks made of silver or glass in which to convey their liquor from home to football game, party, or other entertainment.

One of the intriguing books on decorum written in the later 1800's contains the statement that young ladies never should take more than three glasses of wine, although older females, including professional and married women who are "accustomed to society and habits of affluence," can take five or six glasses. However, hostesses are warned to be cautious about serving wine, "since doing so may start a bad habit or renew a long-controlled passion for alcohol."

The same advisor says it no longer is fashionable to "take wine with each other at dinner," presumably referring to the practice of raising your glass to a dinner partner and enjoying a private sip with him or her.

MAKING THEIR OWN WHISKEY.

READY FOR THE REVENUE AGENTS.

6. Our Business Procedures

Commercial Practices

Businessmen used to be more liberally inclined in the early days. The tavern-keeper every now and then would give everyone a drink on the house, and the saloonkeeper offered a free lunch as an inducement to get customers to come in and buy drinks for cash. The neighborhood baker would give you thirteen rolls when you ordered a dozen; that was known as a baker's dozen.

The general store had a checkerboard where anyone not otherwise occupied could come in for a quiet game, a potbellied stove to warm the players, extra chairs for kibitzers or others to rest in, and an open cracker barrel for the benefit of customers or just plain visitors.

Moreover, if you were known to be a fairly substantial farmer, there was no thought of paying your bills to merchants by the fifteenth of every month. Instead you charged what you bought and the merchant sent a bill once or twice a year, knowing you probably couldn't pay until you had sold your crops or slaughtered your cattle and hogs.

And when you went into the store, there was none of this self-service, get-it-yourself, policy. Instead, the proprietor or a clerk opened the door for you; advised you on the best grade or brand to buy; got the merchandise from the shelf, dusted it off, and brought it to you at the counter; wrapped your parcel with paper and string, and then carried it to the door or out to your carriage for you. If you preferred, the delivery boy brought it to your house and would make several trips a day when necessary.

When you did pay the merchant, you didn't write out and mail an impersonal check. Instead you took the cash down to the store and paid in person, getting a receipt in return. Some merchants had a cage for the bookkeeper or cashier, with a window through which you passed your money. If a child accompanied you when you paid the bill, the storekeeper gave him an apple, cookie, gumdrop,

TAKEN IN TRADE.

THE CHECKER GAME.

THE JEWELER'S SIGN.

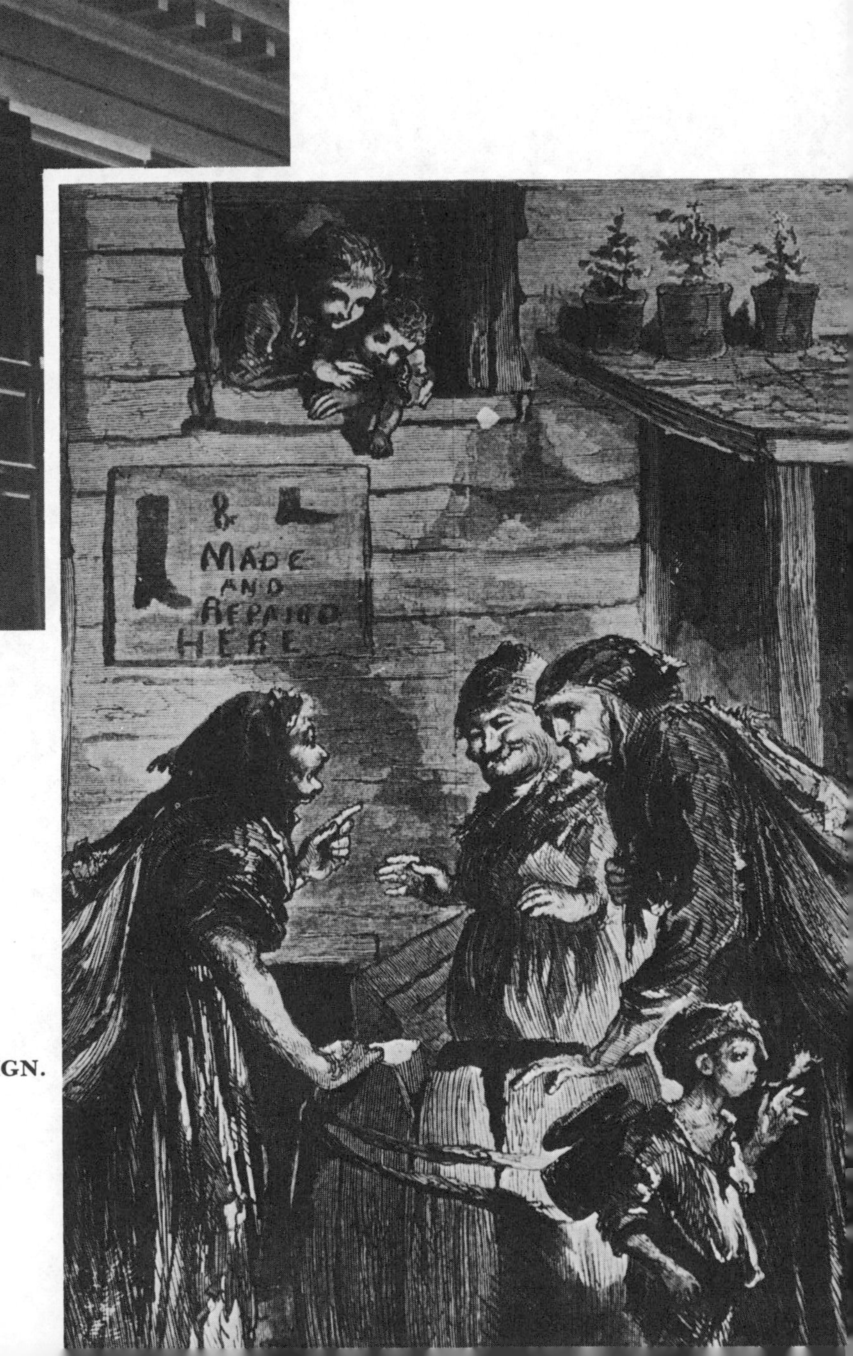

THE BOOTMAKER'S SIGN.

slice of cheese, or other tidbit as a small goodwill offering.

Moreover, you didn't always pay cash. Instead, the proprietor would accept tobacco or corn in lieu of cash. A newspaper editor, perhaps reluctantly, would take a chicken or a sack of potatoes in payment for a year's subscription to his paper. Farmers used to pay for slaves with salt, lard, swine, cows, tobacco, corn, canoes, skins, and other items when cash was scarce.

Because not everyone could read, stores and professional men had outside signs or symbols which identified the type of enterprise carried on inside. There was the cigar store Indian, the barber pole, and the stuffed animal identifying the furrier. Drug stores had a mortar and pestle, veterinarians had a horse, the shoemaker showed a boot or a shoe, and so on. Retail stores had no female employees until close to the beginning of the twentieth century.

One place where present-day policies excel those of former years is in mortgage lending. Mortgages used to be written for a short period of years and the amounts lent were for only a fraction of the total value, so that a man with a mortgage had the threat of foreclosure and possible eviction constantly before him. A mortgage then was looked on as a sort of catastrophe, arranged only as a last resort.

The eight-hour day and forty-hour, five-day work week would have sounded sinful to the Puritans and other early colonists to whom idleness was repulsive. Except for a limited number of holidays, the Sabbath was the only day when steady toil was not expected. A sixty-hour work week was commonplace and a seventy-two hour week was not unheard of for farm and factory workers. One early industrialist explained that his employees might get into serious mischief if turned loose on the streets before they had worked a full twelve-hour day. Sixty and sixty-four hour work weeks were observed in some business as late as 1934 when the Blue Eagle made his first appearance.

A NEWSGIRL.

AN OLD-FASHIONED SALESLADY.

THE PROPRIETOR IN HIS APRON.

A MORTGAGED HOME.

AN EVICTION.

Bulk Buying

The introduction of the paper sack, the cellophane and plastic bag, the glass bottle, and the tin can have brought many changes in the way foods and other commodities are sold by the retail store. In addition, the practice of shopping more frequently, now that it is an easy matter to visit a store several times a week, has led to changes in the way consumers buy.

When he could get to a store only once every two or three weeks and not that often in cold and wet weather, a farmer with a sizable family would come home with a barrel of flour that would last him several months. He also might haul a barrel of kerosene or sugar or whisky if his family needs were great enough.

The store owner bought everything in bulk containers. Other items coming in barrels, customarily holding 30 to 60 gallons or several hundred pounds, were corned beef, smoked pork, beer, vinegar, brandy, salt, and crackers. Corned beef and molasses came in hogsheads which might hold as much as 140 pounds. Wine and oil were received in pipes which held two hogsheads, while beer and wine came in butts of about the same size. Wine also was shipped in large tuns and casks.

Butter came in firkins, rice in tierces, pig's feet in kegs, lard in kilderkins, and salt mackerel in tonnekins. Lard and hams soaked in brine were sold in tubs.

In boxes holding from twenty to sixty pounds the retailer received smoked herring, cheese, crackers, tea, chocolate, soap, soda, saleratus, raisins, and tobacco. Other items came in crocks, pails, jute sacks, and jugs.

Later, in the retail store, cookies and candy were displayed in cartons or caddies to be sold by the pound, while bulk items such as sugar, pepper, salt, tea, coffee, dried fruit, dried peas and beans, rice, butter, and lard were weighed up in one-pound portions.

BULK GOODS FOR SALE.

A WHISKY BARREL.

A CRACKER BOX.

Peddlers and Vendors

The young man who comes to your door today to sell you a magazine subscription is one of the last of a long line of peddlers and vendors who used to supply a large proportion of great-grandma's everyday needs. Because of them, she didn't have to go to the general store more than once every few months, and maybe not that often if the nearest store was too far away.

Peddlers brought her the items that weren't produced by her family—items like needles and pins, hooks and eyes, tableware, tinware, and the like. The peddler carried his wares on his back in a bag or trunk or in a cart, wagon, or boat, taking his goods out where the buyers were, instead of waiting for them to come to him. Some peddlers carried a broad line of items, while others specialized, especially if they stayed near a town of any size. Peddlers also were known as packmen, hawkers, and hucksters.

Some were reliable individuals whose word could be taken without hesitation as to the quality of their wares, while others were as tricky as they come. You didn't dare believe what they said, and you could expect to be cheated unless you kept your eyes wide open.

A vendor was a townsman who either had a stand where he did business every day or else had a hand cart or small wagon with which he toured the neighborhood streets. He sold fish, oysters, fruit, vegetables, popcorn, peanuts, pies, pretzels, and almost anything else that could be moved conveniently. The ice cream vendor is about the only businessman of this kind left on our streets today, although we see an occasional vendor of toys, and ball parks are full of men vending hotdogs, soft drinks, programs, and the like.

A PEDDLER AND HIS SLED.

STREET VENDORS.

A CHESTNUT VENDOR.

Since cash was scarce in the early days, a great deal of peddling was done on a barter basis. A housewife who produced a surplus of homespun or preserves or quilts would trade the excess for salt, pepper, spices, mirrors, pictures, Bibles, books, shoes, or whatever she happened to want at the time. The peddler might give her only a fraction of what her goods were worth, but at least she received something she needed or desired but couldn't or didn't want to make herself.

In addition, people who wanted services of one kind or another—umbrellas mended, clocks repaired, tombstones cut, teeth pulled, and so on—waited until a traveling specialist came along to do the work in their own home.

HOT NUTS FOR SALE.

Transportation

The continuing pressure for greater speed and lower cost has been responsible for many sweeping changes in our transportation customs. Starting with wind, animals, and foot power, we progressed to coal, electricity, gasoline, and diesel oil as sources of power.

Horses, oxen or bulls, mules, and donkeys all played a part in our earlier transportation. Our pioneers rode horseback and sometimes took along a passenger on a pillion. For carrying passengers there were the covered wagon and stagecoach, which often carried freight as well, and the buggy, carriage, chariot, chaise, private coach, surrey, phaeton, brougham, landau, cabriolet, victoria, gig, and buckboard.

People of means used to vie with one another to see who would have the best turned-out rig, the best-dressed coachman, and the snappiest-looking coach dog in horse-and-carriage days.

All deliveries from store to home were made by horse and wagon, and horses also pulled sprinkling carts, fire engines, ambulances, band wagons, and hearses. In the more impressive funerals, hearses were pulled by matched teams of black horses, sometimes preceded by a marching band.

For group travel there also were the horse-drawn hack, omnibus, carry-all, tallyho, and streetcar.

To move freight, and sometimes passengers, too, there were the wagon or wain, which came in many sizes and shapes, the dray, and the cart. The teamster, drayman, carter, hackman, and coachman were all prominent members of society in those days.

When time permitted, coachmen would braid the tails and manes of their horses, and the animals would be protected from summer heat with straw hats through which their ears protruded. To help them cope with flies, the horses wore nets that covered their sides and rump and switched away the pests. Feed bags, whips, hitching posts, and water troughs were other items required in the day of the family horse and carriage.

Coal was the first new fuel to start replacing animals in our transportation scheme, although early steam locomotives and riverboats used wood as fuel. Coal was used to power railroad locomotives, ferryboats, ships, and, in its

AN ACCIDENT.

RIDING ON A PILLION.

A HORSECAR.

early stages, the elevated railroad, but has virtually disappeared in transportation.

Gone with the animals are the corduroy roads made of logs placed at right angle to the direction of travel and the plank roads, not to mention the inns and taverns that were built to accommodate the stagecoach passengers and other travelers.

Most ferries and canals have vanished along with the scows, flatboats, keelboats, and steamships that used to be seen in numbers on our inland waterways.

The interurban electric train has been disappearing rapidly, and street cars, formerly pulled by horses, now are found only in a handful of cities. The open streetcars which were such an attraction in hot weather, except when it rained, and on which young boys used to hitch rides without paying, can be found only in museums.

Another rarity is the sumptuously fitted private railroad car in which tycoons, such as corporation presidents and rail-

A HORSECAR DRIVER.

road executives and high-ranking politicians, used to ride. Even the railroad executives use the airlines these days if they want to get somewhere in a hurry. And needless to say, the automobile has long since replaced the private trains which wealthy parents of a bride used to provide for wedding guests when the ceremony was out of town at a resort or country home.

Bicycles never quite enjoyed the popularity here that they reached on the Continent, but in the late 1800's they were quite the vogue in recreation and sports, as well as for young couples out on a date.

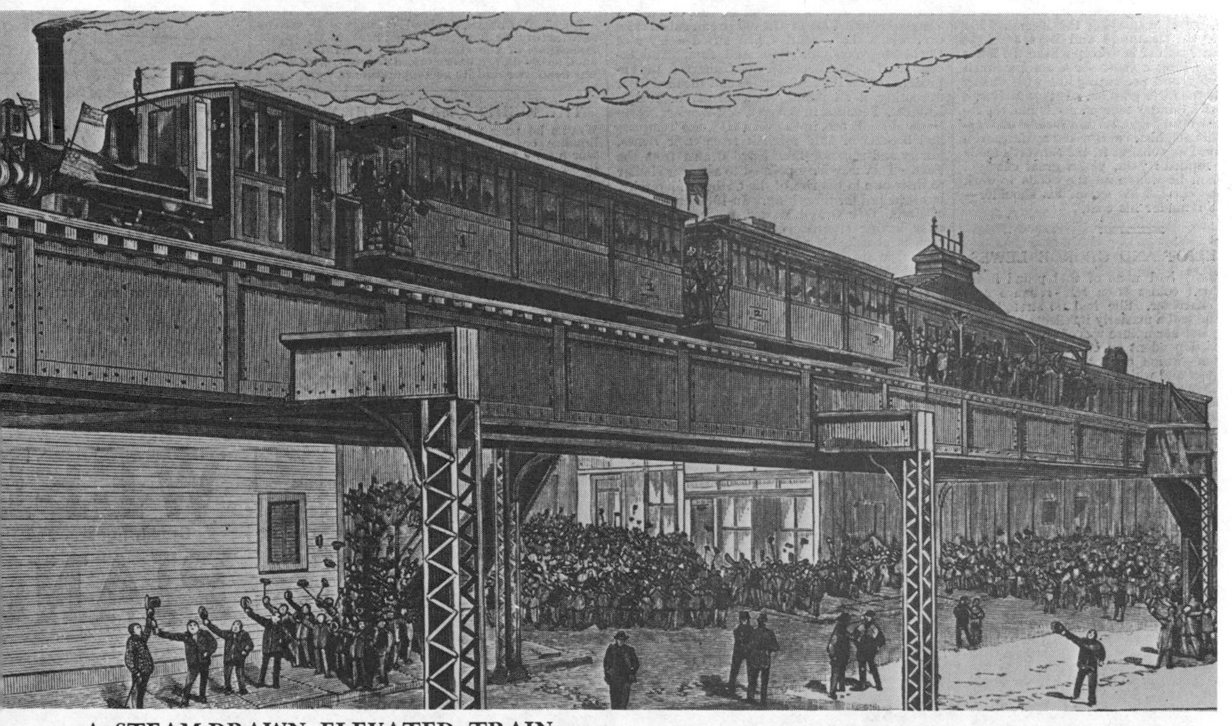

A STEAM-DRAWN ELEVATED TRAIN.

A PAIR OF FAST TROTTERS.

A HORSE-DRAWN AMBULANCE.

A SPRINKLING CART.

A HEARSE PRECEDED BY A BAND.

A HORSE TROUGH.

AN OX WAGON.

GOING TO TOWN.

RIDING IN CLASS.

RIDING ON A COACH.

A SLEIGH RIDE.

A CUTTER AND SLEIGH BELLS.

CYCLING UNDER DIFFICULTIES.

GROUP CYCLING.

DRESSED UP FOR A SPIN IN THE PARK.

A BIG-WHEELED BIKE.

HORSE VERSUS BICYCLE.

NARROW ROADS.

HELD UP BY A MULE.

"WHOA, THERE!"

A COLLISION.

Lodgings

Our earliest hotels—the inns, taverns, ordinaries, and hostels or hostelries, sometimes known as boarding saloons and pothouses—were found along the well traveled roads, at crossroads, and at ferries. They served as local social and drinking centers, in addition to offering food, drink, beds, and accommodations for the horses of travelers.

One tavern sign read:

"Drink for the thirsty.
Food for the hungry.
Lodgings for the weary
and good keeping for the horses."

Their customers came on horseback, in stagecoaches, and in private coaches and sometimes changed horses before resuming their journey.

The taverns usually were some miles apart and, in most places, none too numerous. Thus, it was almost necessary to accommodate all comers, including flunkies and coachmen as well as passengers, since anyone turned away might have to go some considerable distance to obtain food and shelter. The private room was the exception, and guests had to share their room and often their bed with complete strangers.

Tavern operators were regulated rather closely in most communities. Typically, they could not permit drunkenness or excessive drinking and, to that end, were forbidden to sell over one quart of beer or a half pint of wine at one time to one person or to permit continuous tippling by one individual for a period of more than one hour (a half hour, in some places), except with meals.

In one colonial community, tavern keepers could not sell liquors after nine

SPINNING YARNS IN A TAVERN.

p.m., except that they were permitted "to entertain seafarers or land travellers in the night season when they first arrived from a journey or when preparing for a journey the next day, if not disorderly."

The local tavern also was the principal place where plots were hatched, debates held, and duels arranged. It was the headquarters for fox hunters and bull baiters, and the site of auctions, exhibits, elections, dances, business exchanges, and special celebrations. Among the various traveling entertainers who performed in taverns were those staging Punch and Judy shows, lotteries, minstrel shows, and sleight of hand performances, not to mention bell ringers, ventriloquists, and troubadours. Freaks were exhibited and trained animals also.

As urban populations grew, hotels appeared in towns, offering private rooms, but no private baths. A knotted-rope fire escape to be lowered out the window of each room in case of fire was frequently seen in the old two-story hotel buildings. A guest signed his name in a book called a register upon checking in, and a bellboy was summoned by tapping a bell.

A COACH AT THE TAVERN DOOR.

A TAVERN SIGN.

THE OLD HOTEL REGISTER.

7. Our Social Intercourse

Calls and Calling Cards

The personal calling card once played a prominent part in our social lives, and there was a card language that was familiar to all who regarded themselves as ladies and gentlemen. As one social authority put it, "To the cultural disciple of social law, the calling card conveys a subtile and unmistakable intelligence."

Turning down the upper right-hand corner of a card meant it was left in the course of a personal visit to a home.

Turning down the upper left-hand corner meant the owner was expressing felicitations.

Turning down the lower right-hand corner was an expression of condolence.

Turning down the lower left-hand corner meant P.P.C. or "Pour prendre congé," which in turn meant "to say goodbye," presumably when about to leave town for the summer or for all time.

And turning down the whole right end meant that the card was left in person, and not by a coachman, chauffeur, postman, or messenger, for it was entirely proper on certain occasions to "pay a call" by sending a card in an envelope.

One or more cards were left on every call, and calls were made on certain specified occasions. For example, one always left a card for a hostess after a recent visit to her home, and it was imperative that a card be left within four days after taking a meal in a lady's house. One also always left a card, or mailed it, when not attending a reception, the invitation to which did not require a reply.

A card was left for each lady up to three, so if a husband and wife left cards at a home where there were a wife and two daughters, a total of six cards would be left. Only the man left a card for another man, and six was the maximum number of cards to be left on a call to any one-family home.

Cards were left on a special card tray, which the maid or butler held in her or his hand when opening the front door.

TAKING IN A CARD.

AN INFORMAL CHRISTMAS CALL.

The servant always took the card on a tray, never by hand. Between visitors, the tray was left on a small table in the front hall near the door, with a pad of paper and pencil with which to make or leave notes.

Cards always were left at the home of strangers after the first invitation to lunch or dinner, whether or not the invitation was accepted. When a lady was not ready to receive a guest, the servant told the caller that Madam was "not at home." Anyone leaving cards in person always asked if the ladies were at home, except when wishing to end an acquaintance. Merely omitting the question meant the friendship was all over.

Anyone receiving an at-home card with an invitation to a wedding was expected to call on the family of the bride or leave cards within ten days after the wedding.

When a caller left the house at the conclusion of a call, the butler always stood at the door until the caller had reentered his carriage or motor or until he had reached the sidewalk if walking, but when a chauffeur delivered the card the butler could close the door sooner.

It was fashionable to pay "morning" calls on a lady, and they were to be made between two and four o'clock of the afternoon in summer and between two and five o'clock in winter. In addition, many ladies had regular at-home days when they received callers, and one writer recalls that on those days "ladies in their best dresses with trains, bonnets, nose veils, and tight gloves, carrying card cases, would demurely trip from house to house, leaving their broughams and victorias meanwhile to exercise up and down the street."

Calls were paid on New Year's Day, and in New York City the newspapers published lists of ladies expecting callers on that day. Small calling cards were provided for young girls and boys so as to familiarize them with card-leaving etiquette

In addition to at-home and formal receptions, ladies of society gave "kettledrums" which were informal gatherings, held in the daytime, at which light refreshments were served. Guests were expected to stay about half an hour.

When large, formal receptions were held in the daytime, as for weddings or debuts, with shades down or blinds closed and gas lights turned on, guests dressed in formal attire as for an evening function.

A MORNING CALL.

A SOCIETY CALL.

Correspondence

"Reply in your own handwriting" was a phrase that used to be found frequently in want-ads seeking the services of office or clerical personnel, but the typewriter and the various types of bookkeeping, accounting, and data processing machines, plus the general trend toward automation, have de-emphasized good handwriting as a criterion in hiring workers.

The quill pen made from the feather of a goose or other fowl was one of our first writing instruments. Men used to carry penknives, also known as pocketknives, so as to be able to resharpen a quill whenever necessary. On a well appointed desk, along with a quill pen, were an inkhorn, which held homemade ink into which the pen was dipped, and a dish of sand to help dry the ink. One formula for making ink called for "steeping the bark of swamp maple in water, boiling until thick, then diluting with copperas."

In schools, at about the same time, the popular writing equipment before pencils came into general use was the slate and pencil, which had the advantages of being both durable and washable. Our great grandparents all learned to write on slates.

Eventually there came along the

wooden penholder and the separate metal penpoint, which was dipped into an inkwell. The penpoint was dried with a cloth penwiper after use, and the written words were dried by sprinkling sand on them before the blotter was invented. Ink stains, which all too often were found on the fingers, were removed with the aid of pumice stone or soap and water.

It was during the era of the penholder and penpoint, just before we had fountain pens and ballpoints, that a young girl's tresses sometimes got dipped in the inkwell of the desk behind her in school if a mischievous boy was sitting there.

In the day of the quill pen, before envelopes came into general use, many people sealed their letters by folding them twice and sealing the corners with red sealing wax. In those days, authorities on etiquette cautioned readers who used sealing wax to make an even, smoothly finished seal. Readers were advised not to write across a written page as was done by some who sought to save paper in that way.

These same readers were advised also that they should use the third person in writing notes to servants. Thus, one wouldn't say, "Please call me at four o'clock." Instead, the properly worded note would read: "Gracie will please call Mrs. Smith at four o'clock."

Those were the days also of elegant and stilted language in both social and business correspondence. A businessman would write a letter saying, "Yours of the 18th. inst. is safely at hand," meaning "I have received your letter dated March 18."

A letter of appreciation might read: "I

SEALING A LETTER.

A QUILL PEN.

would be wanting in gratitude did I not express to you my thanks for your excellent services to me."

A letter of congratulation would say. "You are married! O, how this sounds! another claims you—another has. all your first thoughts, all your warmest love and sympathies, and life is no longer what it has been to you—a sweet dream, but something real, thoughtful, earnest.

"May there be few of life's storms and tempests for you, but much of its summer of repose and sweet content and may he who has won your pure heart be ever worthy of you. I congratulate you, I bless you, I pray for you."

A letter of proposal would say: "I am conscious that it may be presumptuous for me to address you this note; yet I feel that an honorable declaration of my feelings toward you is due to my own heart and to my future happiness. . . . "

A reply to the letter might have read: "Your note of the 10th reached me duly. Its tone of candor requires from me what it would be improper to refuse—an equally candid answer."

A letter of application would read: "I am desirous of pursuing a mercantile life and write to know if you have any place vacant for a 'new hand.' An answer at your convenience will much oblige, etc."

Communications

When there was no radio or telephone to disseminate news quickly, when newspapers appeared weekly if at all, and before electricity came along to ring bells and sound sirens, other means of reaching the public and attracting attention were required.

To gain the attention of the public-at-large, large bells operated by long ropes were placed on top of town halls, meeting houses, and churches. When bells were not available, alarms were given and attention was attracted by firing cannons, blowing horns, beating drums, and flashing lanterns from the tops of buildings or observation towers. In addition, bellmen, heralds, and town criers carried hand bells to attract attention when proclamations were to be read or alarms sounded.

Out on farms, large bells were placed on the top of tall posts or out-buildings for use in notifying workers that meals were ready or that an emergency had arisen. Or an iron wheel rim was hung from a tripod and hit with a hammer to produce the desired signal.

In place of a pushbutton at the front door, homes had metal knockers or twist bells, which sounded when wound by the caller.

Communication inside the larger home was facilitated by various means, most of them now obsolete. For one thing, there was the speaking tube with built-in whistles at both ends which carried voices from one floor to another, usually from an upstairs hall or bedroom to the kitchen or butler's pantry. From parlor or sitting room to the kitchen was a bell-pull which served to summon the maid or butler. Various other kinds of small bells also were utilized to call servants in the days when they were more numerous than they are today.

Later there sometimes was an elaborate system of bells leading from other rooms to the kitchen, plus an indicator box showing which bell had rung. From dining room to kitchen was a buzzer to summon the maid or cook when her services were needed.

One of the older etiquette books advised taking a bell on picnics for use in calling the frolickers in from the woods and by-paths when the time had come to eat or when it was time to start home.

SIGNALLING BY LANTERN

GIVING A FIRE ALARM.

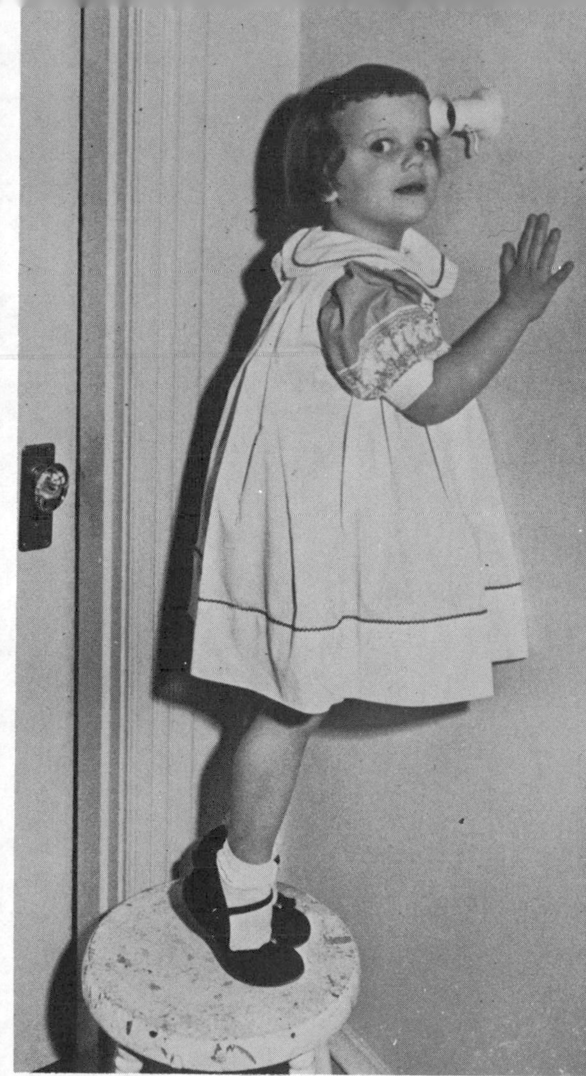

A SPEAKING TUBE.

READING A PROCLAMATION.

GIVING THE ALARM ON HORSEBACK.

SIGNALLING BY MEANS OF COW HORN.

CALLING IN THE FARM HANDS.

AN OLD FARM BELL.

A BELL-PULL.

AN EAR TRUMPET.

A FACTORY BELL.

ANNOUNCING THE ARRIVAL OF A SHIP.

TOLLING THE CHURCH BELL.

CALLING THE LOGGERS BY HORN.

Slang

Our slang words and expressions come and go like the snow. Webster's says slang suggests an appeal to popular fancy and a non-acceptance by authorities. Sometimes, of course, the fastidious authorities are disregarded and what begins as slang ends up in accepted, everyday usage. Such a slang word is "jerk." Webster's did not even list it as late as 1949, but now it looks good for a long run. It means despicable and worthless.

Most of the slang of the period from 1900 to 1930 is already forgotten and most of that in current use is relatively new.

Our most numerous slang words and phrases have been those intended to tell an individual that his company is not wanted. Instead of "go away" and "get lost," which are in use today, we formerly had "23, skidoo," "rous mit yuh," "skedaddle," "go fly a kite," "go to grass," "go roll your hoop," "go soak your head," "go climb a tree," "go chase yourself," "dry up and blow away," and "shoo fly, don't bother me."

"Gump" and "dumdora" are among a list of about 200 slang words meaning dumb or stupid, and there also is a list of phrases that mean the same thing. Among them are: "hurry up and get born," "hang some crepe on your nose, your brains are dead," "nobody home," "nothing upstairs," "he's off his trolley," "he's got bats in his belfry," and "snow again, kid, I've lost your drift."

There was an imposing group of slang phrases referring to human deportment. "Come off your perch," which meant "don't be so superior or high-hat," was typical. Others were: "Set up and take notice," meaning "pay attention"; "wipe off your chin," an appeal for quiet; "let out your back band," an appeal for frankness; "pull down your vest," translated as "behave yourself," while "mind your P's and Q's" meant "be careful."

"You're the limit" meant that you were impossible. "Hold your horses" was an appeal to be more patient. And "you get my goat" meant "you annoy me." "Can it" meant "quit that" or "cut that out." "I'm laughing up my sleeve" was a way of saying you were amused at someone's discomfiture.

There have been many slang names for a drunken person. Among them are: cellar smeller, booze heister, clove hunter, large head, and stew bum. A drunk who was really loaded was said to have a "breath strong enough to carry coal with."

Today we say "that's a bunch of nonsense" or "bunk," but it was not so long ago that they used such expressions as "piffle" and "banana oil." Instead of saying "that's a bunch of malarkey," they said "Tell it to Sweeney," or "Tell it to the Marines," "Says you," "Quit yer kidding," "Oh, yeah!" or "You're talking through your hat."

There also have been many slang terms meaning plain "yes," such as "Yea,

"I LOVE MY WIFE, BUT OH YOU KID!"

"GO FLY A KITE!"

"TWENTY-THREE, SKIDOO!"

bo," "You betcha," "You bet cher life," "You know me, Al," "I'll tell the world," and, not too long ago, "Okie, dokie."

Unusual individuals always have had catchy names applied to them. A fast-living person was a high stepper, a good looking rich boy was a candy kid, a country lad was a brush ape. Of a young man who was highly regarded, they said "He's the cat's pajamas" and "He's the berries" or "the nuts."

A beggar or tramp was known by such names as chronacker, cinder sifter, corner boy, flopper (meaning he begged sitting down), or pillinger. A brakeman on a railroad was a shack or car catcher, a fireman was a tallow pot, and an engineer was referred to as a hogger.

When a girl broke off with a suitor, she gave him the cold shoulder, but when she greeted him warmly she gave him the glad hand. If he was fired from his job, he got it in the neck, and when someone wanted to shake hands with him, they said, "Mitt me."

A speakeasy once was known as a blind pig or blind tiger, a jail was a calaboose,

"YOU'VE GOT BATS IN YOUR BELFRY."

and a police patrol wagon was a hurry wagon.

Two very popular expressions were "Ishka bibble," meaning "I should worry," and "I love my wife but oh! you kid," uttered when a man spotted an unusually attractive girl.

A dollar was a bone or simoleon, money in general was spondulix, and paper money was referred to as toadskins.

An ordinary or slightly uncouth man —the kind we call a guy or fellow today —was known as a gink, bloke, or toff, the latter terms having been borrowed from the British. A lady's man was a lounge lizard, a man addicted to caressing was a canoodler, a man who sought to make love in vestibules was lallygagger, and one who preferred to entertain his girl friend by staying home was a porch warmer or parlor sitter. A girl who sat out at dances—a wall flower—was a chair warmer.

When a pretty girl came along, she heard, instead of wolf whistles, calls such as "Oh, baby!" and "Oh, boy!" She was referred to as a peacherina, a jazz baby, or a sheba, and young men made goo-goo eyes at her. When smooching was in order, one went on a petting party or pitched a little woo, often after making whoopee at a cabaret. The petting often was done in a freezer, a one-time name for an open automobile.

One's head was called a beezer or coco, whiskers were face lace, an elderly man was a bottle nose, and a person who sought to obtain special privilege by private conversation was an earwigger. The head of an organization was known as the main squeeze or the big cheese.

When a man made an extremely humorous remark, you told him, "That would make a stuffed owl laugh," and if he asked a silly question, you replied, "Who struck Billy Patterson?" If he talked your leg off, you said he "talked the soles right off my shoes." When you asked the whereabouts of something you were supposed to know about, you were told it was down the cellar behind the axe.

A burying place for paupers was called "Potter's Field," and the area where houses of ill-repute were located was called the red light district.

A sure thing was a lead pipe cinch, Main Street was the main stem, a man who was all alone was "all by his lonesome," and one who was seriously ill was sick in fourteen languages. When a man forgot a grudge or forgave a mis-service, he was said to have buried the hatchet, and when he went into a tantrum, he was said to be having a conniption fit.

Anything that was out of order was "on the fritz," a barefaced lie was "made up out of whole cloth," and a man who was full of bullet holes was "too full of holes to skin." A soft drink in the early days was a belly washer, a cigarette was a coffin nail, and a toilet seat was an altar or throne. Cheap, sensational books were known as penny dreadfuls and were said to be full of blood-and-thunder. They also were known as dime novels.

Nix meant "no," a portion of food already eaten was "where the flies can't get at it," and a cheap restaurant was a hash house. If you accepted a last-minute, impromptu invitation to dinner at someone's home, you were asked to "take pot luck."

A young man who went calling on his girl wore his Sunday best or his "go-to-meeting" suit. One way to impress a young lady with her lack of appeal was to tell her, "Kiss me, kid, I need a physic." If you uttered a profound truth or made a positive statement, you said, "Put that in your pipe and smoke it." When you felt confident of your opinion, you offered to bet dollars to doughnuts, and if the police suddenly appeared on the scene, you cried out, "Cheese it, the cops."

A snappy reply to an uncomplimentary remark was, "So's your old man!"

Proverbs and Sayings

We have pretty well dropped the once widely practiced habit of quoting old sayings and saws—adages, aphorisms, epigrams, maxims, metaphors, and proverbs—to illustrate or emphasize a point, perhaps because they have become hackneyed or trite from overuse.

Here are some of the aphorisms—short, pithy statements—that used to be heard quite frequently in everyday conversation:

Better late than never.
Finders keepers; losers weepers.
A watched pot never boils.
Look before you leap.
Dog eat dog.
Marry in haste, repent at leisure.
Opportunity knocks but once.
Everything comes to him who waits.
Still waters run deep.
All's fair in love and war.
All's well that ends well.
Pride goeth before a fall.
Out of sight, out of mind.
The fiddler calls the tune.
A new broom sweeps clean.
Barking dogs never bite.
Where there's life, there's hope.
Where there's smoke, there's fire.
There's safety in numbers.
Seeing is believing.
The good die young.
Go whole hog.
Don't carry coals to Newcastle.
Birds of a feather flock together.
Every man has his faults.
Every man has his price.
Manners make the man.
Clothes make the man.
Live and learn.
Silence gives consent.
Nothing ventured, nothing gained.
Spare the rod, spoil the child.
Make hay while the sun shines.
Virtue is its own reward.
If the shoe fits, put it on.

Then there were the maxims—the terse truths or rules:

A stitch in time saves nine.

A burnt child dreads the fire.

If you save the pennies, the dollars will take care of themselves.

Fools rush in where wise men fear to tread.

A chain is only as strong as its weakest link.

Every dog has his day.

Confession is good for the soul.

For want of a nail, the shoe was lost.

Half a loaf is better than none.

It's cheaper to move than pay rent.

His word is as good as his bond.

A thing well bought is half sold.

Where there's a will, there's a way.

Don't put all your eggs in one basket.

A fool and his money are soon parted.

A bird in the hand is worth two in the bush.

It's always darkest just before dawn.

A word to the wise is sufficient.
All that glitters is not gold.
Early to bed, early to rise, makes a man healthy, wealthy, and wise.
The devil finds mischief for idle hands.
Honey catches more flies than vinegar.
Haste makes waste.
Sticks and stones will break my bones, bad words will never hurt me.
Better a big fish in a little pond than a little fish in a big pond.
There's more than one way to skin a cat.
You can take the girl out of the country, but you can't take the country out of the girl.
Necessity is the mother of invention.
One rotten apple can spoil a barrel.
A miss is as good as a mile.
The squeaky wheel gets the grease.
You can't change a leopard's spots.
A child must creep before he learns to walk.
A closed mouth catches no flies.
A rolling stone gathers no moss.
Children and drunken men speak the truth.
Politics makes strange bedfellows.
Don't judge a book by its cover.
One good turn deserves another.
Time and tide wait for no man.
Familiarity breeds contempt.
Two heads are better than one.
You can't draw blood from a turnip.

The apt metaphors which we heard frequently include:

Slow as molasses in January.
Might as well be killed for a sheep as a lamb.
Frisky as a spring lamb.
Frisky as a colt.

A STITCH IN TIME SAVES NINE.

Knee-high to a grasshopper.
Clean as a hound's tooth.
Lies like a trooper.
Slippery as an eel.
Scarce as hen's teeth.
Dead as a doornail.
Quiet as a church mouse.
Grows like a weed.
Easy as rolling off a log.
Ran like a streak of greased lightning.
Faster than a striped ape.
Alike as two peas in a pod.

A wolf in sheep's clothing.

As pure as the driven snow.

He's a dead duck.

Like a bull in a china closet.

Then there were the many epigrams and proverbs—bright, witty, terse thoughts:

Rome was not built in a day.

Set a thief to catch a thief.

Speak well of the dead.

Sufficient for the day is the evil thereof.

Speak of the devil and he will come or send.

Tell me the company you keep, and I will tell you what you are.

The higher the rise, the greater the fall.

The pitcher that goes to the well too often gets broken at last.

The proof of the pudding is in the eating.

The silent dog is the first to bite.

There are no gains without pains.

Valor would fight but discretion runs away.

When the cat's away, the mice will play.

When poverty comes in the door, love leaps out the window.

You can't make a silk purse out of a sow's ear.

Cut your coat according to your cloth.

You never miss the water until the well runs dry.

The way to a man's heart is through his stomach.

You can lead a horse to water, but you can't make him drink.

What's sauce for the goose is sauce for the gander.

A place for everything, and everything in its place.

Sing before breakfast, cry before night.

Procrastination is the thief of time.

He has a white elephant on his hands.

Red at night, sailor's delight; red in the morning, sailors take warning.

Rain before seven, clear before eleven.

One man's meat is another man's poison.

Fine feathers don't make fine birds.

Absence makes the heart grow fonder.

There's no fool like an old fool.

Don't count your chickens before they are hatched.

It's good riddance for bad rubbish.

He's barking up the wrong tree.

The wolf is at the door.

Give him enough rope and he'll hang himself.

She drew his chestnuts out of the fire.

It depends on whose ox is being gored.

Let him stew in his own juices.

Old soldiers never die; they simply fade away.

Put your nose to the grindstone.

Those who play with fire are sure to get burnt.

You're making a mountain out of a molehill.

He had to eat crow.

A bad penny always turns up.

You can't burn your candle at both ends.

A wise man reflecteth before he speaks.

As you make your bed, so shall you lie in it.

In Rome, do as the Romans do.

Faint heart never won fair lady.

God helps them who help themselves.

Don't look a gift horse in the mouth.

Possession is nine points of the law.

He's got him over a barrel.

8. Our Crime and Punishment

The Law

Among our best known sets of old laws are the Blue Laws first laid down in Connecticut in the 1600's and later copied in part by other colonies. They mainly were intended to promote church attendance and discourage luxury, ranging well beyond the present-day Blue Laws which strive to limit business activity on the Sabbath.

Extravagance in dress was condemned both in New England and Virginia. The Puritans forbade silk hoods and "great sleeves," as well as face powders and eyebrow darkeners. Massachusetts had a law that said:

The court, taking into consideration the great, superfluous, and unnecessary expenses occasioned by reason of some new and immodest fashions, as also the ordinary wearing of gold, silver, and silk laces, girdles, hatbands, et cetera, hath therefore ordered that no person, man or woman, shall hereafter make or buy any apparel, either wool, silk, or linen, with any lace on it, silver, gold, silk, or thread under penalty of forfeiture of such clothes.

Also that no person, man or woman, shall make or buy any slashed clothes, other than one slash in each sleeve and one in the back; also all cutworks, embroidered, or needlework caps, bands, and rayles are forbidden hereafter to be made and worn under the aforesaid penalty; also all gold and silver girdles, hatbands, belts, ruffs, and beaver hats are prohibited to be bought and worn hereafter under the same penalty.

Turning to compulsory church attendance, there was a law in Virginia in the early 1600's that said:

Every man and woman shall repair in the morning to the divine service and sermon preached upon the Sabbath Day and in the afternoon to divine service and catechising upon pain, for the first fault, to lose their provisions and the allowance for the whole week following; for the second, to lose the allowance and be whipped; and for the third, to suffer death.

However, the supreme penalty probably was never inflicted. There is a record of one court decision fining a man fifty pounds of tobacco and whipping him for not attending divine service on Sunday.

In Virginia there was also a law that a man would lose his wages if he did not attend divine service everyday, be whipped the second time he committed this offense, and be condemned to the galleys for a third offense.

In Connecticut at that same time the death penalty was prescribed for kidnaping a man, being a witch, adultery, rape, perversion, incest, blaspheming the name of God, worshiping other than God, and being convicted of burglary or robbery for the third time.

Working on Sunday—profaning the Sabbath—was another serious offense and one law stipulated that:

> Whoever shall profane the Lord's Day or any part of it, either by sinful service work or by unlawful sport, recreation, or otherwise, whether willfully or in a careless neglect, shall be duly punished by fine, imprisonment, or corporally, according to the nature and measure of the sin and offense. But if the court upon examination find that the sin was proudly and with a high hand committed against the known command and authority of the Blessed God, such a person therein disparaging and reproaching the Lord shall be put to death, that all others may feare and shun rebellious courses.

Another Blue Law provided that, "if a child above sixteen shall curse or smite his father or mother, it shall be put to death unless it is proved that the parent has been unchristian, negligent, or cruel." Ordinary swearing and public kissing were punishable by placing the culprit in the stocks, and then whipping him if he committed a third offense.

The master of a family was required to "catechise his children and servants at least once a week in the grounds and principles of religion."

No unmarried young man, no servant, and no public officer was pèrmitted to keep house for himself without permission of the town, and no master of a family was permitted to give entrance or habitation to any young man to sojourn in his family except with permission of the town.

As far west as Ohio, where the Blue Laws were not too well-known, it was forbidden by law at one time to play billiards or sell a deck of cards.

In one New England town, just prior to 1700, public housekeepers were required not to "permit, suffer, or house any playing of dice, cards, tables, quoits, loggets, bowls, ninepins, or billiards in the house, yard, gardens, or backsides." Presumably this restriction was intended to discourage people from gambling and from frittering away their time on nonproductive pursuits.

Home Punishments

The forms of punishments that we use today are, on the whole, far more simple and humane than those formerly used. The practice of inflicting corporal punishment has been discontinued, except in extreme cases and where individuals inflict punishment on others outside the law.

In the home, youthful offenders were punished by taking them behind the woodshed or out behind the barn and applying a vigorous right hand or a strap, belt, paddle, switch, stick, or other instrument to the individual's backside. Spankings are still administered in some families, but the place of punishment

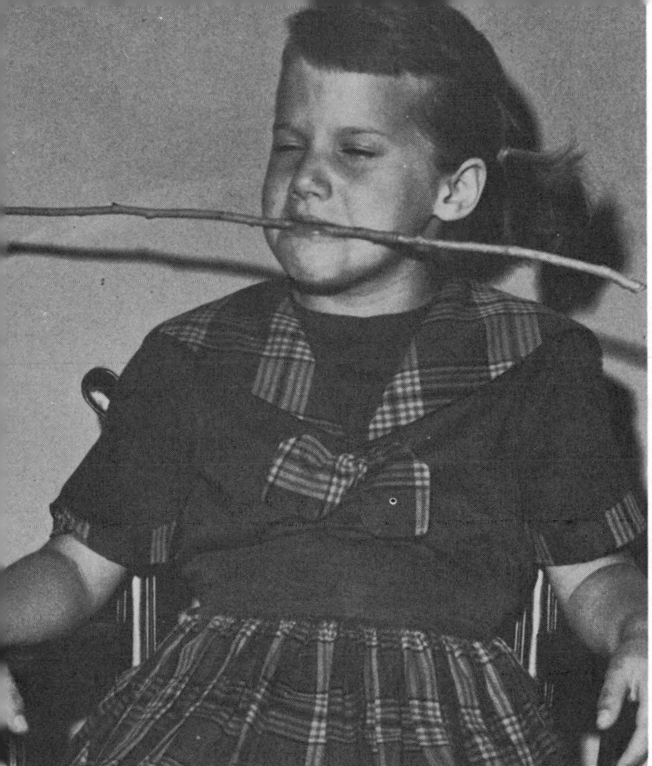

A SPLIT STICK ON HER TONGUE.

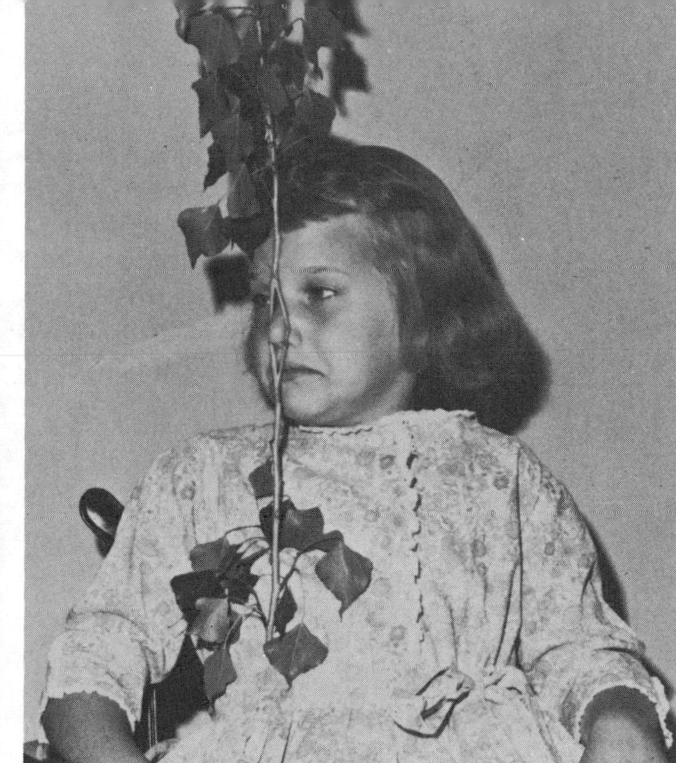

A SPLIT SAPLING ON HER NOSE.

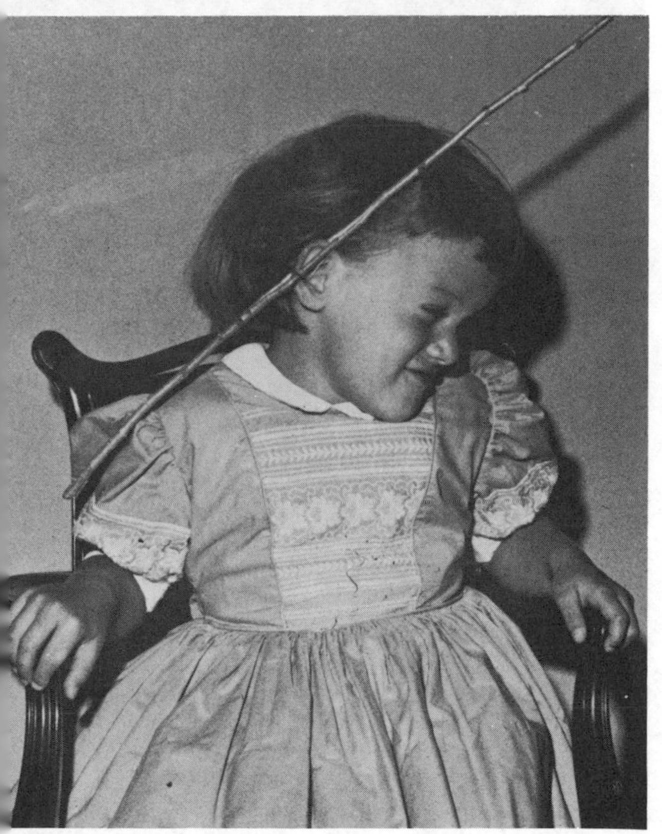

A STICK ON HER EAR.

now is the basement or a bedroom because so few families have woodsheds or barns.

Other household punishments consisted of boxing the ears of the culprit if he was impudent or disobedient, washing out his mouth with soap and water if he told a lie or uttered a naughty word, slapping his face if he made faces at one of his elders, or sending him to his room. If the punisher were a female, she sometimes tapped the head of the errant child with a thimble. In extreme cases, he or she was put on a temporary diet of bread and water or even made to go without a meal.

The modern tendency is to replace these punishments with persuasive reasoning or with reprimands.

Schoolroom Punishment

In the classroom, too, punishments and disciplinary methods have changed radically. Whereas it used to be common practice to whip recalcitrant boys with a switch or sting their hands with a ferule, meaning a rod or ruler, it now is against the law in many places for a teacher to touch a child for disciplinary purposes, let alone resort to corporal punishment. If any spanking is permitted, the principal often is the only one authorized to administer it.

Indeed, it now is considered poor teaching practice to ridicule a child or humiliate him in front of other children. Well-trained teachers state that they can maintain order without resorting to such tactics. They rely on the use of reason, appeals to pride, and so on.

Thus, the boy who whispers or creates disorder no longer is made to sit under his desk or sit tied to a confederate by a rope. Nor is he required to sit at the same desk with a girl. The practice of requiring a culprit to stand on a box or in a corner with his face to the wall or to sit there on a stool wearing a dunce cap is also passé.

This being the case, it is hardly necessary to add that other forms of physical punishment, such as washing out a pupil's mouth with soap, shaking him, compelling him to squat on the floor with his finger on the head of a nail, and fitting him with a wooden gag, similar to a bit worn by horses, are used no more. This is also true of applying a finger pillory or thumb-stock to one of the child's fingers and pinching the end of his nose, the end of his tongue, or the lobe of an ear with a cleft stick. The finger pillory was a device that fitted around the fingers and kept them immovable.

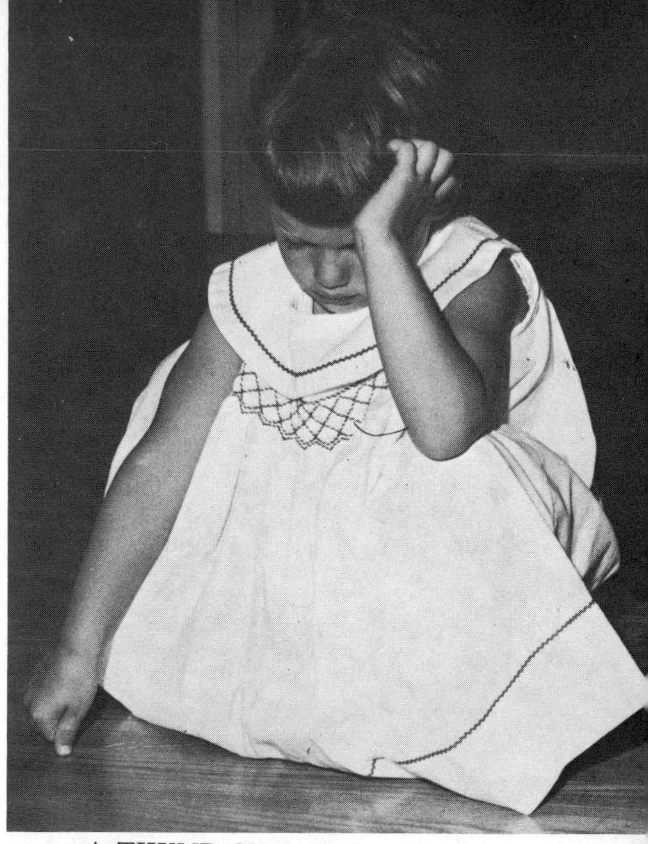

A THUMB ON A NAIL.

Since these rather drastic and sometimes painful penalties were often applied for relatively harmless forms of misbehavior, such as throwing spitballs, passing notes, whispering, sassing the teacher, and hiding his or her spectacles, it is just as well that they have been abolished.

STANDING ON A BOX.

Church Punishment

The churches had their own special forms of punishment, usually for sexual offenses, drunkenness, or dishonesty.

One punishment consisted of requiring the guilty party to stand during the service on a repentance stool, which was about one foot higher than an ordinary seat, thus placing the individual in full view of the congregation.

Church members who were morally culpable were compelled to appear in church on the Sabbath wrapped in a white sheet or wearing a white robe, sometimes holding a white rod or staff. In some places, sackcloth was substituted for the white robe, thus adding the discomfort to humiliation.

Another form of punishment consisted of having a guilty party stand up and confess his sin before the congregation. Individuals who made a habit of drinking to excess were subjected to strong criticism from their wives, their pastors, and town officials. It was not uncommon to see a frequent offender, under great pressure from friends and relatives, rise up in church and take the pledge, which meant voicing a promise to refrain from alcoholic beverages in the future. Some persons took the pledge numerous times before it stuck or they became discouraged.

TAKING THE PLEDGE.

Personal Punishment

Extra-judicial or personal punishments also have undergone considerable change, but they are no less violent; they merely have taken on a new form.

A man no longer challenges another to a duel when he thinks his honor is at stake, because dueling has been made illegal. Men do not horsewhip each other, because they no longer own horsewhips. They don't cane each other, because they've stopped carrying canes. Bumping heads together to penalize two foolish or stubborn individuals now is a figure of speech, instead of a reality as it was some years back.

Vicious hand-to-hand combat in which the adversaries maimed each other by biting off noses, ears, and lips is seldom heard of in this enlightened age, but we still do have the kick in the pants, the slap in the face, and the punch in the jaw or nose. When extreme measures are taken, the revolver and the knife have replaced the horsewhip and other earlier weapons.

Punishments by groups of self-appointed vigilantes have declined, although occasional incidents are reported, so there is less hanging, tar-and-feathering, and riding out of town on a rail. These days we never hear of a man being dragged behind a horse on the end of a rope or of another old-time form of punishment—forcing a man to run the gauntlet, which meant running between two facing rows of people, each of whom beat him with a club, jabbed him with a spear, or switched him with a stick as he passed by.

Gone also are such maritime practices as spread-eagling a troublemaker to the shrouds with arms and legs extended; keel-hauling, which meant hauling a man under the keel of a ship at the end of a rope, or walking the plank, in which a blindfolded man with his hands tied behind him was compelled to walk overboard to his death in mid-ocean. These practices were discontinued with the disappearance of the pirate ship and the old wooden sailing vessel. Putting a man in chains is still practiced on vessels that do not have a brig, but flogging with a cat-o'-nine-tails is a thing of the past. The unions simply do not permit it.

SPREAD-EAGLED.

BUMPING HEADS TOGETHER.

RUNNING THE GAUNTLET.

A HORSEWHIPPING.

A DUEL.

KEEL-HAULING.

IN CHAINS.

A FLOGGING.

A CANING.

HUNG BY A MOB.

PUNISHMENT BY VIGILANTES.

A HANGING.

A GUILLOTINE.

A MASS HANGING.

A GAUNTLET OF SPEARS.

WALKING OVER HOT PLOWSHARES.

RIDING BACKWARD THROUGH TOWN.

A COWARD.

A FEMININE CULPRIT.

THIEVES.

A DRUNK.

PARADING AN OFFENDER IN A CAGE.

AN ADULTERESS.

9. Official Punishment

One who is convicted of a serious crime today knows that his punishment will consist of either a fine, imprisonment with or without hard labor, or death, usually by the electric chair or the gas chamber. In olden times, however, the variety of punishments was considerably greater and often more cruel. Less drastic sentences for offenses like drunkenness or disorderly conduct included such comparatively harmless penalties as being required to keep a bridge in repair, saw firewood for the town hall for a year, fall on one's knees and beg forgiveness, or submit to being preached at in court.

At the other extreme were punishments such as being beheaded by an axe or the guillotine and being placed in a gibbet, as formerly practiced in England and elsewhere, and such early American punishments as having one's tongue pierced with a red-hot rod or knife, having one's ears nailed to a pillory and then cut off or cropped upon release, and being drawn or dragged to the gallows at the back of a cart prior to hanging.

A gibbet was a metal frame which surrounded the body of a person who had been hanged. It had a ring on top so it could be suspended from a tree or pole, thus keeping the body on display as a warning to other criminals.

The practice of ear-cropping is said to have been partly responsible for the large number of wigs worn in early days, because a wig effectively covered up the loss of all or part of an ear as punishment for a past crime.

One form of punishment that involved extreme mental cruelty consisted of sentencing a man to be hanged and then reprieving him on the gallows at the last moment, provided he agreed to serve as official hangman for the community in the future.

Other punishments on record consisted of sentencing a deserter from the army to work with negroes for two years, compelling a smuggler to jump three times from the yardarm of a ship prior to whipping, and tying a soldier found guilty of a sex offense in a canvas sack and *casting him into a river.* One man was fastened to a stake near a gallows with a bundle of rods under his arms, a bridle or gag in his mouth, and a sign on his chest describing his crime, which was blasphemy. Another man was tied to a stake while shots were fired over his head. A woman was placed in the stocks in New England for raising her hand against her husband.

All of these punishments and others like them were prescribed by the courts or military authorities. In some places, whipping and other physical punishments were reserved for servants, slaves, and persons "of low order." When necessary, gentlemen were punished with fines, which could be paid in tobacco or corn, rather than cash. In at least one instance, a "gentleman" who was found guilty of stealing from Indians was officially referred to in court by his first name, instead of being called mister, thus making him eligible for whipping.

Humiliation, ridicule, and mockery were regarded as effective criminal deterrents, or at least as suitable penalties for many offenses. One form of humiliation was branding culprits with letters that stood for various crimes or offenses. Thus, a thief would be branded with a T, a hog stealer with an H, a malefactor with an M, and so on. The brands were applied either on the forehead, chest, shoulder, thumb, or hand, and indelible ink sometimes was substituted for the branding iron.

Less painful, but just as humiliating, was the practice of sentencing an individual to wear a sign that told of his offense. A drunk would be compelled to wear a sign containing the word *drunk* or a large D for a month or more. A coward would have to wear a large C or the whole word on a sign, a blasphemer would wear a B, or he might be required to stand in court with a sign in his hat telling of his offense. An adulteress would have to wear an A, sometimes in scarlet, and a woman who consorted with an Indian was sentenced to wear the figure of an Indian in red cloth on her arm for a year.

A drunk, and there apparently were many of them, was sometimes compelled to wear a barrel in place of his clothing. The barrel was known also as a drunkard's cloak. Extreme drunkenness was penalized also by forbidding the individual to hold office or to vote in local elections and by forcing him or her to drink a quantity of salt water mixed with lamp oil.

Even paupers were penalized for the crime of being poor. In some places they were required to wear a badge on their shoulder, just as a thief wore a sign, and were whipped if they failed to wear it.

Cheating merchants received special punishment by being exposed to their own wares. A seller of spoiled fish would have a necklace of dead smelts placed around his neck, a baker guilty of short weight would have a loaf of bread hung from his neck, and a grocer who sold adulterated spices would be placed in the stocks and the adulterated spices burned under his nose. An errant carpenter was sentenced to build stocks and then was their first occupant.

Convicted criminals were sometimes placed in cold, damp dungeons, compelled to wear an iron collar the rest of their lives, drummed out of town, banished from the colony, placed on a treadmill to grind corn by footpower, or tied to the back of a cart and whipped continuously as it moved about town. The chain gang, in which groups of criminals are chained together to work on roads or other public works, has not yet vanished from this country.

One popular way of humiliating a culprit was to parade him through town riding backward on a horse with hands tied behind him or in a clumsy, wooden cage like an animal. A horse thief, in addition to being branded, sometimes was required to sit publicly on a wooden horse for a stated period of time. This could be quite uncomfortable because the board usually had sharp edges and it was customary to attach fifty-pound weights to each foot. In frontier days, of course, horse thieves usually were hanged with little ceremony or delay.

Liars, blasphemers, and cursers were punished by putting their tongue through a split stick or a growing branch, by boring their tongue with a red hot poker, or by placing a gag in their mouth.

Impecunious individuals who could not pay a fine were sometimes sold as servants or slaves for a fixed period. Debtors were sent to prison. The term of indenture for a slave would be extended for sexual misconduct, while a freeman who seduced another man's slave was sometimes required to serve her master during the period when she was unable to work on account of childbirth. In some instances, slaves were freed if their master misused them sexually.

Punishments frequently were combined. Thus, a culprit might be fined, whipped, and have an ear cropped for malicious speeches about the government. Someone always was thinking up a new form of punishment in the days when jails were few and expensive to maintain. In Connecticut, prisoners were charged for the meals they ate while in jail.

The Brank

Scolding or reviling, which meant uttering ill-tempered abuse, were ranked as very serious offenses in olden days, and for those convicted of either offense there were special devices for punishment. One of the less known—not often used in this country—was an iron frame, called a brank, which surrounded the head of the culprit and had a triangular piece of metal that entered the mouth, thus effectively discouraging the impulse to scold or even to talk in a normal manner. Branks also were known as scold's helmets and dame's bridles.

Other devices used to penalize scolds were the ducking stool and the cucking stool. The former, sometimes called a castigatory or trebucket, was a chair with arms and a metal band that passed in front of the occupant to keep him or her from falling out or escaping. It was mounted on one end of a beam which rested on a fulcrum like a seesaw, permitting officials at the other end to alternately lower and raise the stool and thus duck the scolder in a pond or river.

The cucking stool, also called a coucking stool or a penance stool, was primarily for use on dry land. With or without a gag, the occupant was required to sit in it without hat and shoes in the doorway of her home or other public spot, to be pelted and jeered at. Sometimes the stool and its occupant were placed on a cart or tumbrel and paraded through the town and then dunked in a pool.

Both stools were also used for other types of offenders, including drunks, thieves, merchants giving short weight or misrepresenting their merchandise, and unruly paupers.

Instead of being placed on stools, scolds and other offenders sometimes were required to stand on large blocks four feet high, exposed to taunts, rotten eggs, and mockery.

The Whipping Post

The list of humiliating punishments included having one's hair or beard shaved off, being required to whip other more serious offenders, and being compelled to stand by a whipping post with back bared and a whip hanging over one's head, presumably as a threat of more drastic punishment for any future offense.

However, the whipping post was used freely in early colonial days for offenses such as stealing, blaspheming, cheating the public, pretending love, selling rum to the Indians, sleeping during church, wife beating, and other similar offenses. Both men and women were lashed publicly, with their hands tied to a ring in the post above their heads. They commonly received from ten to forty lashes "well laid on" by a cat-o'-nine-tails, also called a tattling stick. The cat consisted of a stock or handle about twenty inches long with nine rawhide lashes, each about one and one-half inches wide, attached to one end.

Several states still have laws specifying whipping as a punishment for certain offenses, including scolding and wife beating, but that form of punishment is seldom applied.

The Pillory and the Stocks

Popular devices for public punishment in the early days were the pillory, or neck-stretcher, and the stocks, which supplemented each other in that the pillory confined the neck and hands of the culprit whereas the stocks customarily confined the feet and sometimes the hands as well.

A WHIPPING POST.

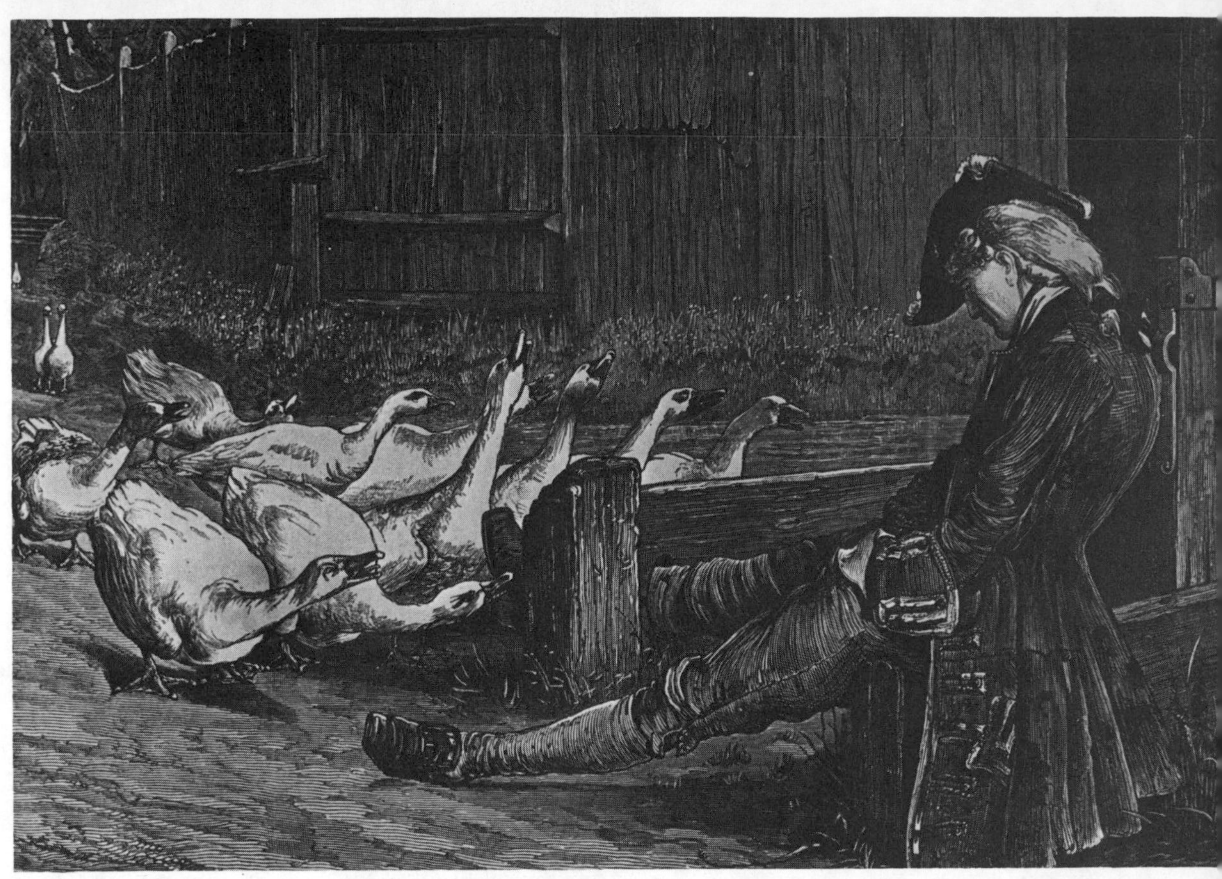

A POOR GOOSE.

OUT OF ACTION.

HELPLESS TO PROTECT HIMSELF.

OBJECTS OF INTEREST.

In each case, a split board with a hinge at one end had holes through which the extremities might be placed for confinement. The stocks and pillory usually were located in the center of town or near the jail, where passersby could, if they desired, taunt and harass the unfortunates confined therein. In some places, the pillory was located on a platform up above the stocks and whipping post and was reached by a ladder.

When none of those devices was available, criminals were effectively immobilized by means of fetters or bilboes, which were iron bars that shackled the feet and prevented escape. If fetters were not available, there was a jougs, a metal collar which could be opened to fit around the neck of a culprit. To it was attached a short chain, which in turn could be fastened to a wall or post in a public place.

If the authorities were solicitous about the comfort of persons placed in the stocks, they would build a roof overhead to protect the victim from the elements or else postpone the time of confinement until bad weather had passed on.